Date D

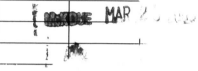
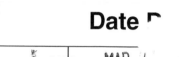

MAR

PECULIAR POWER

PECULIAR POWER

A Quaker

Woman

Preacher in

Eighteenth-

Century

America

Smithsonian

Institution

Press

✳

Washington

and London

Cristine Levenduski

Portions of Chapters 2 and 4 appeared in "'Remarkable
Experiences in the Life of Elizabeth Ashbridge': Por-
traying the Public Woman in Spiritual Autobiography,"
Women's Studies 19 (1991): 247–81. They are reprinted
with the publisher's permission.

Editor: Jenelle Walthour
Designer: Lisa Vann

Library of Congress Cataloging-in-Publication Data
Levenduski, Cristine M.
    Peculiar power : a Quaker woman preacher in
eighteenth-century America / Cristine Levenduski.
        p.   cm.
    Includes bibliographical references and index.
    ISBN 1-56098-670-0 (case : alk. paper)
    1. Ashbridge, Elizabeth, 1713–1755. 2. Society of
Friends—United States—Clergy—Biography.
3. Quaker women—United States—Biography.
I. Title.
BX7795.A7L48   1996
289.6'092—dc20
    [B]   95-48862

British Library Cataloguing-in-Publication Data is
available

Manufactured in the United States of America
03 02 01 00 99 98 97 96   5 4 3 2 1

⊗ The paper used in this publication meets the
minimum requirements of the American National
Standard for Information Sciences—Permanence of
Paper for Printed Library Materials ANSI Z39.48-1984.

For
Mary
and
Daniel
Levenduski

Contents

Acknowledgments

Teachers, friends, colleagues, and students, too numerous to mention here, have provided encouragement and valuable criticism throughout the various stages of this project, and I am thankful to each of them. I owe special thanks to Roland Delattre and Karal Ann Marling, who read early versions of this project. Amy Lang provided a critical eye and a supportive shoulder throughout its later stages, and I am most grateful for her guidance.

My richest source of information on Elizabeth Ashbridge has been Daniel Shea. I am grateful to him for his initial recovery of her story, his insightful reading of her narrative, his extensive archival work on its textual history, and most especially, for his willingness to share his work with me.

Words of thanks are inadequate to acknowledge my debts to Edward Griffin. He has willingly—even cheerfully—read many drafts of the manuscript, early and late, and his insightful critiques and suggestions have only improved the final version. My heartfelt thanks to him for his extraordinary generosity as a scholar, teacher, mentor, and friend.

Librarians at the University of Minnesota, Emory University, the Historical Society of Pennsylvania, the American Antiquarian Society, and the British Museum have facilitated my research. Financial support from the University of Minnesota American Studies Program made early work on this project possible, and Emory University graciously funded the project's latter stages.

Mark Hirsch guided this book through the publication process.

His enthusiasm and wise counsel made the final steps more pleasant than I had imagined possible.

Finally, the greatest debts in any project with the longevity of this one are personal. For the many forms of love and support they have provided and continue to provide, this book is dedicated to my parents.

PECULIAR POWER

1

Introduction

Elizabeth Sampson Sullivan Ashbridge, a prominent eighteenth-century Quaker minister, nearly vanished from the American historical record not long after her death in 1755. References to her in colonial records are few, and until very recently, she was virtually unmentioned by historians of early America. Most of the details of her extraordinary life survive only in her autobiographical narrative, a text largely ignored by literary scholars and, until the 1990s, unavailable to modern readers. However, renewed interest in Ashbridge has been sparked by Daniel B. Shea's discussion of the narrative in his path-breaking study of American spiritual autobiography and in his introduction to the recent edition of her narrative, heretofore the only significant commentary on Ashbridge.

Peculiar Power: A Quaker Woman Preacher in Eighteenth-Century America participates in the recovery of Ashbridge as an important figure in American literary and cultural history. It is not, however, a biography of this amazing woman. Owing to the paucity of extant extratextual historical information about her and barring the discovery of significant new evidence, no full biography of Ashbridge can yet be written. I have thus placed her autobiography—her *own* version of her life and times—in its literary, historical, and social contexts, demonstrating how a single powerful document can broaden and deepen our understanding of early America and also open new perspectives on the subtle, complex art of life-writing. Although she left only one document, long hidden away on the shelves of a few libraries, its recovery now enables us to hear again a voice speaking dramatically and with uncommon power to the concerns of her times as well as our own.

Among the most salient of these concerns is the attitude of a democratic society toward pluralism, an issue made manifest by the Quaker presence in colonial America from the earliest days of British settlement. Long a classic, John Woolman's *Journal* has undoubtedly held its honored place in American literature not only for its lucid style but also for its compression of the ethos of the Society of Friends and the Quaker spirit of cultural critique into one narrative. Woolman's experiences appear to supply the perfect synecdoche for life outside of America's burgeoning democratic mainstream. The story of Elizabeth Ashbridge, however, complementing Woolman's in many respects, offers even richer possibilities as synecdoche than does Woolman's, particularly in the political realm. As a woman, an immigrant, and a convert, she was more an outsider than he, and her narrative thus underscores even more clearly than his the capacity of marginalized groups to push early America's mainstream political culture to confront pluralism's place in a democratic culture. One aim of *Peculiar Power* is to highlight the Quaker woman's experience in this context of early American pluralism, arguing for the continued importance of this figure in later American literary and cultural history.

Even when sketched in skeletal form, the details of Ashbridge's life and adventures demonstrate the difficulty of ignoring her story. Born in England in 1713, she was the only child of Thomas Sampson, a ship's surgeon, and Mary Sampson, a devout member of the Anglican church. Against her parents' wishes, at age fourteen she eloped with an impoverished stocking weaver, only to find herself widowed five months later. Estranged from her father because of her marriage, she lived for five years with relatives in Ireland until, as a last act of rebellion, she decided to emigrate to the American colonies. While preparing for her move, she was kidnapped by an unscrupulous woman in the business of buying and selling indentured servants. After escaping, Elizabeth returned, presumably unwittingly, to the ship on which she had been held captive and set sail for the American colonies. During the voyage she overheard a band of mutinous Irish servants plotting to seize control of the ship. By informing the captain, she succeeded in preventing the mutiny; he rewarded her by forcing her to sign illegal indentureship papers, binding her to a four-year contract, which he later sold to a cruel master in New York.

Elizabeth's term of indenture, marked by numerous hardships, included a "difference" with her master that resulted in her narrow escape from a beating by the town whipper summoned to deliver her punishment. During her servitude, she flirted with a career on the New York stage, but her singing and dancing abilities notwithstanding, she abandoned it out of respect for what she assumed would be the wishes of her father. After earning enough money through needlework to pay off the last year of her indentureship, Elizabeth married a schoolteacher named Sullivan, who fell in love with her because of her singing and dancing, but for whom she initially felt no love.

During this second marriage, Elizabeth, unsatisfied by her Anglican upbringing, searched for a religious center to her life. While visiting relatives in Pennsylvania, she became convinced of the Quaker truth. Sullivan, threatened by her conversion, frantically removed her from the site of her newfound strength and forced her to lead the life of a vagabond, following him around the colonies. She persisted in her Quaker practice, however, and eventually became a minister. After much physical, mental, and emotional abuse from Sullivan, occasioned by her new activities as a Quaker preacher, Elizabeth finally found some small measure of peace and stability within their marriage. She too became a schoolmaster, and Sullivan began to show interest in Quakerism.

Sullivan, however, cut short this period of relative calm. While inebriated one night, he enlisted in the army, left their New Jersey home, and found himself posted to Cuba. His enlistment notwithstanding, he refused when called upon to fight, choosing instead to adopt the Quaker practice of pacificism. As a consequence, he was beaten so severely and suffered so much physical abuse that he was sent to a hospital near London, where he died nine months later. Widowed again, Elizabeth remained a schoolteacher and also sold her needlework until she paid all of Sullivan's considerable debts, an obligation she was not required by law to undertake.

Five years after Sullivan's death, Elizabeth married again, this time to Aaron Ashbridge, a prominent member of a staunch Quaker family in Chester County, Pennsylvania. With her membership in the

Ashbridge family and her growing distinction as a traveling Quaker minister, she gained a firm position within the Pennsylvania Quaker community. Yet after fewer than seven years with her new status, Elizabeth Ashbridge in 1753 abandoned the security of family and community and left Pennsylvania to preach in Ireland. Contracting a severe illness, she died there on May 16, 1755, at the home of Robert Lecky and was buried at the Friends' burial ground, Ballybromhill, in County Carlow, Ireland.

Her legacy to literature is her personal narrative, known in several versions as her "Remarkable Experiences." In writing her autobiography, Elizabeth Ashbridge participated in the tradition of Quaker ministers writing narratives of their coming to the Quaker truth to provide other Friends with encouragement and with examples to emulate. The story Ashbridge tells, however, bears little similarity to those of her contemporaries, and the uniqueness of her story makes her case a difficult one. She writes from a position outside the cultural mainstream that forms much of our understanding of the intellectual life of early America. Many studies of eighteenth-century thought and literature are dominated by the figures of Jonathan Edwards, a representative of the evangelical congregationalist, and Benjamin Franklin, an example of the rational Deist. When the Quaker experience is considered, John Woolman usually serves as its sole proponent. Women's voices, if they sound at all, are heard primarily through the late eighteenth-century letters of such famous figures as Abigail Adams. While Ashbridge shares something with all of these writers, her experiences elude neat categorization. In her difference lies her importance.

While Ashbridge's position as a Quaker minister enabled her to speak, the multivocality of her text makes it much more than a preacher's conversion narrative. She writes not only as a Quaker but also as a woman, an indentured servant, and an immigrant. Moreover, her narrative provides exceptions to commonplace assumptions about early America, thus revealing problems for the modern reader who might attempt to study any one of these experiences in isolation. Ashbridge reminds us that Quakers were not always born Quakers but sometimes came to their faith later in life; that although eighteenth-century women usually were kept from public roles, some assumed public positions equal to those of men; that although most indentured servants remained poor, some rose above mean beginnings to positions of prominence; and that not all immigrants to the American colonies considered themselves cut off from their homeland—Ashbridge's community spanned the Atlantic, including England, Ireland, and the West Indies, as well as the American colonies.

In speaking from the margins of early American life, Ashbridge provides a perspective not found among the voices of the dominant culture. Hers is the story of one woman situated on the edges of society, every avenue to the center closed to her, who doggedly searches for a way to survive on the periphery. Then, having prevailed but refusing to be content with mere survival, she works to show others her methods. In sharing what she has learned in her struggle, she empowers and authorizes herself as a potential force in the culture around her. Destined to remain forever marginalized, Ashbridge nevertheless found a way to exert power by helping to articulate and to disseminate a cultural vision, with the tenets of Quakerism at its core, that is at once appealing to the dominant culture yet subversive enough of cultural norms to change the shape of the world around her.

✳

Elizabeth Ashbridge's "Remarkable Experiences" carries weight beyond the story of one woman's life.[1] The intermingling of her personal history with the corporate history of the Society of Friends illustrates how the Quakers' definition of themselves as culturally "other" both limited but also empowered them. Just as Ashbridge eventually wrested from Sullivan control of her own religious practices, the Quakers, despite their emphasis on simplicity and pacifism, refused to be passive participants in their own marginalization. By emphasizing the material trappings of their lives, they controlled the terms of their otherness, and from a position of dissent and opposition they turned their peculiarities into powerful instruments of influence on the dominant culture.

In part, Quakers influenced by example. From the beginnings of British American culture, Quakers and Puritans established a tradition of opposition that, as R. Laurence Moore argues, "encouraged people to express their most cherished convictions in the language of dissent," which "did a great deal to expose the shabbiness and arrogance of the culture surrounding them and contributed a fair measure to whatever success the American system has had" (xi–xii). In Moore's formulation, American religious culture has always emphasized conflict, with outsiders continually posing challenges to the dominant group. The outcome of religious struggle has been determined as much by "the importance that opposing groups attach to one another" as by the reality of the power balance. Consequently, groups like the Quakers "who play the role of outsiders can wield enormous public influence," disproportionate to their numbers—influence "that the alleged insiders are powerless to block" (xiii). In colonial America, Quakers self-consciously placed themselves in the role of outsiders, thereby simultaneously encouraging the dominant culture to perceive them as threats to the system while positioning themselves to influence the shape of early America.

Other historians agree that Quakers exercised considerable influence, but argue that it was hardly subtle and indirect. Robert Kelley's theory of American political history, for example, views Quakers as important agents of social action. Understanding early America as "a kind of national folk theater in which ancient, almost tribal enemies contend," and where conflicts among "ethnic groups, styles of life, ideologies, moral values and religious faiths" are as powerful as economic interests (vi), Kelley argues that democratic political ideals originated not within the dominant society but precisely within groups such as the Quakers, who struggled to maintain a minority identity: "in their parochial self-interest they [had] need of the protection of such ideals" (27). By emphasizing the potential universality of the Inner Light, Quakers were predisposed to democratic models of government. Moreover, their testimony of equality promoted pluralism in early American culture. Their self-consciously constructed peculiarity highlighted cultural diversity wherever they settled, and such diversity, Kelley contends, made the middle colonies, with their high Quaker population, the fulcrum for the emerging American political system:

> Precisely because they were so culturally pluralistic—a confusion of tongues, religions, and peoples—within [Pennsylvania and New York] we see emerging, for the first time, essentially modern, mass-based two party systems. (50)

Where colonists "had a plentiful supply of adversaries within their own borders," they formed political parties based on ethnic and religious heritages that identified traditional enemies (101). Quakers' visible markers of otherness situated them in the thick of this process.

By defining themselves through opposition and dissent, Quakers like Elizabeth Ashbridge placed themselves on the margins of eighteenth-century society. Paradoxically, in maintaining their distinctiveness, they also participated in defining and shaping the cultural mainstream that had to contend with their otherness. As a people, they provided early evidence that, at least in the culturally diverse middle colonies, the melting pot did not mitigate religious and ethnic differences. In some instances, in fact, the opposite seemed to be true. Frederick Tolles suggests that in early Pennsylvania the American experience reinforced rather than erased group identity, making the colony's political history "a story of continuous struggle, not primarily between social classes or economic groups, but among cultural and religious blocs." "Selective interaction" and cultural borrowing among these blocs—not assimilation—became common practice ("Culture" 135–36).

Within this atmosphere of cultural give-and-take, the Quakers created and maintained a sense of otherness, thereby preserving a culture distinct enough to have something to offer to non-Quakers. In the early eighteenth century, as they came to realize that theirs would never be the dominant culture in America, Quakers chose not to settle for passivity and impotence but instead found ways to spread their beliefs from the cultural margins. Doing so forced them to invent creative forms of political activity that at once protected their principles and their group identity, while also effecting change in the dominant culture around them.

Through the case of Elizabeth Ashbridge, this pattern in Quaker cultural history becomes visible in a single life. As she seeks to reconcile her marginalization and her power within her autobiography, she reenacts on an individual level the corporate history of Quakerism. Her eighteenth-century story recalls the beginnings of the drama of the Quaker tradition in the seventeenth century and participates in the projection of that tradition's principles into the nineteenth century. In recovering her story, we recover much more than a solitary, feeble voice

on the lunatic fringes of eighteenth-century culture. Ashbridge speaks
with a powerful voice. Although she led a life restricted at every turn,
her influence in her community was strong, allowing her to provide a
model of female empowerment that resonates through later American
culture. As a representative of the broader tradition of Quaker cultural
influence, her voice must be heard if we are to understand the pluralism of eighteenth-century America.

✴

Precisely because of its multivocality and its importance for an understanding of cultural pluralism in colonial America, Ashbridge's narrative is appropriately poised for inclusion in contemporary studies of
early America and of women's autobiography. First published in 1774,
her narrative circulated within the Quaker community throughout the
nineteenth century and the early twentieth century. It appeared in at
least thirteen printed versions with varying titles, including *A Sketch of
the Early Life of Elizabeth Ashbridge, Remarkable Experiences in the Life
of Elizabeth Ashbridge: A True Account,* and the more common *Some
Account of the Fore-Part of the Life of Elizabeth Ashbridge.* In addition, at
least twelve manuscript versions, copied in several hands, are extant.
Outside the Quaker community the text was virtually unknown until
Daniel Shea's discussion of it in his 1968 study, *Spiritual Autobiography
in Early America.* Subsequently, an excerpt of the text was included in
a 1978 classroom anthology, *America in Literature,* edited by David
Levin and Theodore Gross. More recently, however, the text—
excerpted in both the Norton and the Heath anthologies of American
literature, as well as in the new Penguin anthology, *Early American
Writing*—has become part of the emerging revisionist canon of early
American literature. The authoritative edition of the entire narrative,
edited by Daniel Shea, is now available in *Journeys in New Worlds:
Early American Women's Narratives.*

The enterprise of studying women's personal narratives as separate and distinct from the wider tradition of American autobiography
is of comparatively recent origin. Scholars have first had to recognize
the ways in which women's narratives have been excluded from criticism of American autobiography and then to understand the differ-

ences that separate personal narratives by women from those written by men. Much of the criticism of this genre, therefore, has necessarily been aimed at definition, with critics assembling lists of criteria that distinguish women's autobiography from men's. In the growing body of theory on women's personal writing, Ashbridge's narrative is particularly useful both as a reification of and a challenge to current understandings of the gendered nature of autobiographical writing.

It has become a critical commonplace that personal writing by women tends toward particular subjects and a distinctive style: while men's narratives characteristically focus on their public lives, women's narratives emphasize the personal and domestic side of their activities and identities; while men's narratives are chronological and continuous, women's narratives are stylistically more episodic and fragmentary, and they often follow a nonlinear pattern of organization (Jelinek, *Tradition* xiii). Indeed, these "fissures of female discontinuity" sometimes become so large that the self created in women's texts is decentered or even absent, as opposed to the more organic and centered figure in men's autobiography (Benstock 20–21). Where men's narratives stress accomplishments, women's narratives stress relationships with family, friends, or some significant "other" (Stoneburner 9), consistently inscribing a "sort of evolution and delineation of an identity by way of alterity" (Mason 41). This identity comes in part from women's propensity to see "herself through the imagined (or real) gaze of another" (Culley 9). Often this relational emphasis is so strong that the woman autobiographer's sense of herself emerges as a collective identity, where a cultural group becomes the "source of strength and transformation" in her development (Friedman 39).

Ashbridge's narrative reflects each of these broad characteristics in some way, but her text is more important—and indeed more interesting—for the ways it also challenges or complicates each of these criteria, thereby forcing readers to move beyond what have become the common expectations of the genre. For example, in Ashbridge's use of her private history of suffering and abuse to legitimize her later prestige, the narrative blurs the boundaries between public and private for women empowered within the semipublic sphere of a marginalized group like the Quakers. Ashbridge reminds her readers that women's everyday experiences were not always domestic and that the Quaker home was often an arena for the discussion of public issues. Similarly, by presenting her story in chronological sequence, Ashbridge provides an exception to the generalization that women's narratives are necessarily sites of fissures and discontinuity. If her narrative is fragmentary, it is so only in that she stops writing before describing her life as a prominent member of a Quaker community and a Quaker family. Closure exists, however, in her decision to end her narrative with the death of Sullivan, forcing her readers to ask whether this tactic is merely evidence of the definition of self through the presence of an "other," or a highly sophisticated narrative strategy that allows her to most effectively demonstrate the exemplary nature of her faith through the influence she had on her second husband. At every turn, Ashbridge's narrative challenges insufficiently examined generalizations about the content and the narrative style believed conventional or even appropriate for women's autobiography. Her text serves as a stellar example of a woman's autobiography that at some points "ventriloquates male ideologies of gender while it allows alternative discourses of 'experience' to erupt at the margins of meaning" (Nussbaum, "Commonplaces" 149).

The extraordinary experiences that "erupt" in Ashbridge's story raise questions for the modern reader about possible influences on her narrative art. As she put into print the events of her past, what forces helped to shape her memories? Her acting career, brief though it was, makes literature one likely influence. Indeed, the opening pages of her story read like a chapter from a Richardsonian novel! Her connections within the transatlantic community of Friends would certainly have afforded her access to contemporary British literature. If so, can the similarities between the details and the tone of her story and such novels as *Pamela* (1740–41) or *Clarissa* (1747–48) be only coincidence?[2] Suggesting such parallels is, of course, mere speculation, but the resemblances are striking nonetheless. Rather than undermining the power or credibility of Ashbridge's narrative, these similarities heighten the complexity of her story, posing further challenges to easy assumptions about her life and her text. The circumstances of her life simply will not allow facile conclusions, nor will the power of the voice with which she speaks allow us to diminish the strength of the woman behind it. The self that Ashbridge creates in her narrative can only be understood as the site of intersecting voices, all of which must be heard to understand her story.

✳

This study of Elizabeth Ashbridge begins with a reading of her narrative—*her* statement of what it meant to be a woman, a disobedient daughter, a wife, an immigrant, an indentured servant, and a Quaker in the eighteenth century. However, with its historical accuracy suspect, as is the case with all personal narratives, the narrative raises endless questions about the use of such a text in constructing cultural understandings of early America. Without any extensive extratextual historical record of her life, her biography cannot serve as the starting point. Since almost all of what we know of her stems from her autobiography, that single narrative remains the only textual focus from which work on the case of Elizabeth Ashbridge can proceed. New angles of vision must be explored to provide evidence that reinforces the power of the autobiographical truth inherent within her story.

Seeing the text as object, this study uses Ashbridge's narrative as the focus for analysis by picturing it from multiple angles, viewing it through a variety of historical and disciplinary lenses, bringing it into focus against several different backgrounds. In its most straightforward context, her narrative fits within the literary and spiritual tradition of Quaker ministers writing to document their exemplary piety and their coming to the Quaker truth. Ashbridge, chronicling her conversion to Quakerism, demonstrates that the extraordinary efficacy of the Inner Light within her life ultimately empowered her within the Quaker community. The circuitous and often rocky path that she describes on her way to this ascent, however, can be understood only against the historical background of seventeenth-century Quaker persecutions, a story that itself leads to yet another context—the problems incurred throughout colonial American culture by women asserting themselves in the public life. A woman required by the spirit to speak (and, indeed, to write) of the workings of the Inner Light in a society that prescribed her constraint and silence prompts questions about the tensions arising from her predicament and their effect on her understanding of herself as a character in her autobiography. Through a close reading of the internal evidence in the narrative, combined with the insights of recent theories of women's creation of self in autobiography, these questions can begin to be addressed.

But even as tentative answers emerge, other pressing questions arise about the parallels between Ashbridge's sense of self and the institutional identity of the Society of Friends. By shifting the angle of vision from questions of individual identity to the corporate formation of Quaker identity—specifically to the conflict between the Quaker need to be at once outsiders and yet successful within the dominant culture—the tensions in Ashbridge's own life come into sharper focus. From this sight line, we can begin to understand the seemingly paradoxical coexistence between her sense of herself as a figure on the margins of society and her power and prestige within the Quaker meeting. By shifting the vantage point forward chronologically to examine how the figure of the Quaker woman is inscribed in the American literary tradition, the case of Elizabeth Ashbridge brings into focus the ways in which those on the margins of American society can influence, and sometimes even wield power, within the dominant culture.

What becomes clear through each of these lenses is a different part of the picture of Elizabeth Ashbridge. Each angle of vision, overlapping with another, yields new, and sometimes conflicting, perspectives about her and her cultural context. The collage that results from the combined foci offers an understanding of her life that is at once more complex and more complete than the mere sum of its multiple vantage points might imply. As the portrait of Ashbridge that emerges here illustrates, the life lived on the margins of early American society was filled with conflicts and complexities that do much to further our knowledge of everyday life in colonial America.

The following chapters explore the case of Elizabeth Ashbridge by subjecting her narrative to scrutiny from this series of vantage points. Chapter 2 places her narrative within the historical context of the seventeenth-century persecutions of Quakers throughout the colonies. It argues that to understand not only the corporate history of Quakerism in the eighteenth century but also the specific events in Ashbridge's life, we need to consider the horrors of those seventeenth-century experiences. Alive in the cultural imaginations of her second husband and his non-Quaker friends, stories of the abuses of Quakers in the seventeenth-century provided them a context from which to justify their inhumane treatment of Ashbridge. Similarly, the connections among the early Quakers, the antinomians led by Anne Hutchinson, and those infamous women accused of witchcraft in seventeenth-century Massachusetts provide a context within which to understand the attitudes about public women that haunted Ashbridge nearly a century later.

Moving from the historical past to Ashbridge's contemporary present, Chapter 3 demonstrates the great discrepancy between her narrative portrayal of herself as hapless victim and her actual life circumstances when she wrote her autobiography. By choosing to end her text at the point where she learns that her traumatic life with her abusive second husband is over, she effectively avoids discussion of her growing fame and prestige as a traveling Quaker preacher, as well as any description of her rise in class and comfort as Aaron Ashbridge's wife. This chapter uses extratextual historical evidence to construct a sense of her later life of relative privilege, and it explores the question of why she chose to exclude details of this portion of her life from her narrative.

Chapter 4 provides a close reading of the textual evidence that Ashbridge offers about her "remarkable experiences." Beginning with the generic conventions of conversion narratives written by other prominent ministers to document their exemplary piety, the chapter demonstrates how her narrative fails to fit within the confines of the genre and instead moves toward something more akin to autobiography. With a double purpose evident as she writes—the public function of the conversion narrative and the more private need to find unity in her life—Ashbridge chooses the themes of alienation and separation as a structural device for her text.

Building on the reading of her text in Chapter 4, Chapter 5 juxtaposes Ashbridge's narrative with John Woolman's journal. Examining the events these two autobiographers chose to include in their texts, their modes of narrating these events, and their use of the material culture of their everyday lives as codes for their growing commitment to their faith, this chapter argues that the striking differences between these two narratives result from a combination of the authors' gender differences and their divergent cultural positions, shaped by differences in the circumstances that brought them to the power of the Inner Light and into the Quaker community.

Chapter 6 moves into the nineteenth century to examine the ways in which the figure of the Quaker woman recurs in the American literary tradition. Through analysis of several works of early American fiction—John Neal's *Rachel Dyer,* Eliza Buckminster Lee's *Naomi,* Rebecca Beach's *The Puritan and the Quaker,* as well as the better known *Uncle Tom's Cabin* by Harriet Beecher Stowe, *Life in the Iron Mills* by Elizabeth Harding Davis, and *Work: A Story of Experience* by Louisa May Alcott—this chapter argues that the fictional representations of the Quaker woman sprinkled liberally throughout nineteenth-century American novels are encoded with certain feminist values that present challenges to nineteenth-century cultural norms. Relying on the historical drama surrounding Quaker women, as well as on the prominence of Quaker women in nineteenth-century reform movements, these novelists recognized the subversive power of the Quaker tradition—particularly when it is embodied in women. They used this tradition to present alternative cultural visions that challenged dominant cultural norms. As Ashbridge's narrative presages, in this body of literature the Quaker woman becomes much more than a quaint oddity and passive victim. Instead, like Ashbridge, she finds agency, actively exerting power and influence from her position of otherness to affect the shape of early American culture.

2

"Better Be Hanged"

Quakers,

Preachers,

and Public

Women

Elizabeth Sullivan's conversion to Quakerism profoundly changed her life. For the first time since childhood she felt that she had found the true religion, and this conviction gave her life a centeredness she had never before known. Yet her husband treated her Quakerism like a disease to be treated and cured. On the advice of an Anglican priest, Mr. Sullivan sought to remove her from Pennsylvania, the source, he believed, of her contamination. Elizabeth, fearing his choleric temper and desiring to be an obedient wife, went with him quietly.

Having traveled all day on foot, Elizabeth was relieved when she and her husband stopped for the night at a tavern in Wilmington, Delaware. But she was also apprehensive, knowing that popular opinion regarding Quakers agreed with that of her husband. No sooner had they entered the tavern than Mr. Sullivan began to tell fellow travelers and townspeople, hungry for diversion, that his wife had become a Quaker. Throughout dinner he regaled them with stories of her extended visit to her relatives and of his horror at their reunion when she addressed him with the dreaded Quaker "thee." He won their sympathies when he told them of her former career in the theater and of how he had fallen in love with her because of her skill as a dancer, though she now refused to sing or to dance.

As her husband spoke, Elizabeth Sullivan saw the other tavern guests' sympathetic reactions to his story, and her anxiety grew, for she knew that her convictions and those of her husband would soon clash. When a musician among the group, evidently sharing Sullivan's view of Quakerism as a curable ailment, offered to hasten her "recovery" by fetching his fiddle and starting a dance, Elizabeth knew that the confrontation was at hand.

When the fiddler started playing, Sullivan, taking his wife's hand, said, "Come my Dear, shake off that Gloom, & let's have a civil Dance, you would now and then when you were a good Church-woman, & that's better than a Stiff Quaker." Wary of her husband's volatile temper, Elizabeth begged to be excused from the dance, but firm in his belief that with one dance he could bring an end to her foolishness, Sullivan insisted. He pulled her from the tavern bench and, when she remained still, dragged her across the floor until tears flowed from her eyes. The fiddler, seeing her tears, mercifully stopped playing and said to Sullivan, "I'll play no more, Let your wife alone" (E. Ashbridge 162).[1]

This 1736 incident in the Wilmington tavern left its mark upon Sullivan's wife, and fifteen years later, when Elizabeth Sullivan Ashbridge wrote the story of her conversion to Quakerism, she remembered it vividly. This incident became a prime illustration of the conflict between her Quaker convincement and her marriage. Although her beliefs triggered a long series of abuses from her husband, the scene in the tavern is the first, the most detailed, and also the most dramatic story she tells.

The tavern incident is powerful because it resonates with a long history of anti-Quaker sentiment in American culture. All the actors in this scene—Elizabeth Sullivan, her husband, and the musician—are aware of this tradition; Elizabeth Ashbridge, the autobiographer, evokes it in her retrospective narrative; and for readers, this tradition places her narrative within a cultural context that locates Quakers in general and female Quaker preachers in particular on the fringes of acceptable society. So prevalent was this anti-Quaker mythology in the daily lives of Ashbridge and of her contemporaries that she feels no need to explain it, even though it provides an important and necessary subtext for her story. Her retelling of the Wilmington tavern incident must be read in this context in order to understand its bearing on her autobiography.

Mr. Sullivan had more at stake in the tavern that night in 1736 than his desire to have a carefree wife who enjoyed dancing with him. Sullivan, like the others in the tavern, knew early eighteenth-century

Quakers as "peculiar people," individuals set apart from the dominant culture by language, dress, behavior, and beliefs. By forcing Elizabeth to dance, he tried to rescue her from "otherness" and marginalization in a society valuing communal unity and conformity. Having tried unsuccessfully to sway her from her newly found Quaker convictions, he turned to physical means—removing her from the site of her conversion, preventing her from attending Quaker meetings, and forcing her to dance—all attempts to pluck her from the margins of peculiarity and place her within the mainstream. These were the acts of a desperate man threatened by the prospect of losing his wife to the supposed Quaker deviance that he and his neighbors had heard about, as well as by the recognition that his own life would be tainted by her beliefs and actions. That night Elizabeth Sullivan suffered not only from a harsh husband but also from an unrelenting cultural mythology.

✳

Early America's popular perception of Quakers as a "peculiar people" came in part from the Quakers' own actions.[2] Their plain style of dress, their use of "thee" and "thou" to address all persons regardless of class or title, and their refusal to take oaths or to remove their hats as a sign of deference visibly set them apart from members of the dominant culture in British North America, as well as in Europe. In many communities these practices occasioned only curiosity and gave rise to the image of members of the Society of Friends as dull, drab, and sober folks, an image that persists throughout the literature of late-nineteenth- and twentieth-century America.[3] Many who knew the early Quakers, however, saw them as anything but dull and quiet. On both sides of the Atlantic, the perceived peculiarity of the Quakers threatened members of the dominant culture, and their fears inspired voluminous published attacks charging the Quakers with a wide variety of wrongdoings.[4]

Among the earliest anti-Quaker publications was John Gilpin's *The Quakers Shaken* (1653). Having once been a Quaker himself, Gilpin, using his experiences to illustrate the aberrant conduct of the Quakers in meetings, argues that this behavior is evidence of demonic possession (Cherry 12). Charges of demonic intervention in the Quakers' actions became commonplace in seventeenth-century anti-Quaker literature. By 1690 Cotton Mather needed only a brief reference to the "strange Quaking, which look'd so like a Diabolical Possession" to remind his congregation of the Quakers' role in perpetuating the evils affecting the Puritan community (Silverman 88). Other seventeenth-century tracts were more imaginative in the evils they attributed to the Quakers. Labeling them "Spawn of Romish Frogs, Jesuits and Franciscan Friars," William Prynne's *The Quakers Unmasked* (1655) finds Quakers in league with the Pope in a plan to overthrow the English crown (Cherry 13). While most of these anti-Quaker tracts were printed in England, copies of the pamphlets circulated freely in New England as early as 1653, and British colonists soon began to write some of their own. Thomas Welde, a Massachusetts minister and participant in Anne Hutchinson's famous trial, wrote two anti-Quaker tracts in 1653 and 1654, and Samuel Eaton, brother of the governor of New Haven, penned *The Quaker Confuted* in 1654 (Jones 29–30). With the proliferation of such writings in both England and New England, the people of British North America had ready access to the vehemence of popular English anti-Quaker sentiment well before any Quakers actually set foot in Massachusetts Bay Colony.

Not surprisingly, when Mary Austin and Anne Fisher arrived in Boston Harbor on board *The Swallow* in 1656, they were not welcomed. The leaders of Massachusetts Bay Colony had enough problems without the added complication of these two Quaker women. Only twenty-five years after arriving in Massachusetts Bay, the Puritans knew already that the reality of their settlement paled by comparison with the original intent of the community's founders, and they struggled to regain the strength and intensity of the original vision. Massachusetts popular sentiment, fueled by anti-Quaker mythology, thus viewed these interlopers with hostility. They were a threat to religious purity and homogeneity and a further unnecessary hindrance to the Puritan errand.

The Massachusetts officers ordered by Deputy Governor Richard Bellingham to examine Fisher and Austin upon their arrival found them to "hold many very dangerous, heretical and blasphemous Opinions" and to be in Boston expressly to propagate "their said errors and heresies, bringing with them, and spreading here sundry Books, wherein are contained many most corrupt, heretical and blasphemous Doctrines, contrary to the truth of the Gospel" (Norton 5). As punishment for this heresy, the court ordered the women imprisoned, their books burned, and the ship's captain held financially responsible for the cost of their imprisonment and for transporting them away from the colony (Norton 6). After accusing these women of being witches, the officials began to search them inhumanely for witches' marks. Humphrey Norton, a contemporary chronicler of these events and a Quaker who was himself branded with an "H" for heresy, reported that, with both women and men present, the officials

> stript them stark naked, not missing head nor feet, searching
> betwixt their toes, and amongst their hair . . . and abusing their
> bodies more than modesty can mention, in so much that Anne who
> was a married woman, and had born 5 children said, That she had
> not suffered so much in the birth of them all, as she had done
> under their barbarous and cruel hands. (7)

This was not an isolated incident. The records of the Massachusetts Bay Colony and the seventeenth-century Quaker chroniclers document numerous instances of such persecution. Nonetheless, the Quakers kept coming. No sooner were Austin and Fisher expelled from Massachusetts than others arrived in larger numbers.[5] Massachusetts laws became progressively more severe in an attempt to stem the tide of heretics. Within five years, punishment for Quakerism increased beyond mere imprisonment and deportation to whipping, ear cropping, and, by 1658, banishment upon pain of death for repeat offenders.

Among the most famous of these repeat offenders were Mary Dyer, William Robinson, and Marmaduke Stephenson, who returned to Boston in 1659 after each had been banished from the colony on at least one previous visit. Along with a larger group of Quakers intent upon challenging the Massachusetts law, this trio was arrested and jailed and, perhaps because of their renown among the Quaker community, selected from among the larger group to be hanged on Boston Common. The spectacle that surrounded their hanging guaranteed that the event would become a part of the colony's popular history. Dyer, Robinson, and Stephenson walked to the gallows in a paradelike atmosphere. Several drummers rhythmically drowned out any heretical preaching that they might attempt, and bands of armed men on horseback lined the route to keep them away from the crowds of onlookers (Burrough 24). Even as these Quakers were going to their death, colonial officials feared their perceived power to corrupt the Puritan theocracy in Massachusetts.

Most memorable in this event is the image of Mary Dyer, who stood with hands and feet bound while her companions were hanged and then courageously climbed the ladder to her own scheduled death:

> She stept up the Ladder and had her Coats tyed about her feet, and the Rope put about her neck; and as the Hangman was ready to turn her off, they cryed out, Stop, for she was Reprieved, and having loosed her feet, bad her come down; but she was not forward to come down, but stood still, saying, She was there willing to suffer as her Brethren did, unless they would null their wicked Law, but they pulled her down, and a day or two after carried her by force out of Town. (Burrough 25)

As Rufus Jones has shown, her pardon was not the sudden conciliation by colonial officials that it seemed, but rather part of a carefully scripted piece of high drama. The official records of Massachusetts Colony from 18 October 1659, eight days prior to the hanging, explain the plan:

> It is ordered that the said Mary Dyer shall have liberty for forty-eight hours to depart out of this Jurisdiction, after which time, being found therein, she is to be forthwith executed. And it is further ordered that she shall be carried to the place of execution and there to stand upon the Gallows with a rope about her neck until the Rest be executed; and then to return to the prison and remain as aforesaid. (Jones 86)

Although the court's purpose behind these theatrics remains unexplained, their concessions probably reflected the lack of unanimity among officials concerning Quaker executions more than any sympathy for Dyer. Whatever their reasons, their actions placed Dyer firmly within the cultural imagination of the seventeenth-century colonists, so that when she once again returned to Boston in 1660 and Governor

John Endecott again ordered her hanged, she was already a known figure throughout the colonies. This time the sentence was carried out,
and Dyer's martyrdom was complete. Humphrey Atherton, a Boston
official, is reported to have said scoffingly of her hanging body, "She
hangs there as a flag!" (Jones 89). His observation was prophetic, for
Dyer, more than any other Quaker, became the symbol of Quaker
martyrdom for later generations.

Dyer's hanging, along with those of Stephenson and Robinson,
captured the attention of King Charles II, who, after his restoration to
the throne in 1660, brought an end to Quaker executions. His order
was issued in response to a petition signed by Quakers banished from
Massachusetts that outlined their sufferings. Tallying the numbers of
Quakers who had been beaten, fined, imprisoned, sold as servants, and
injured, this petition sought the king's intervention on the basis of the
Puritans' hypocrisy.[6] The Quakers' actions, the petitioners argued, mir-
rored those of the Puritans themselves only a few years earlier, yet
"they have ignorantly condemned themselves in the same things for
which they have judged others" (Burrough 5).

While the king's order successfully put an end to the hangings,
other brutal persecutions continued. As if in reaction to Charles's
order, the Massachusetts General Court immediately instituted in 1661
the Cart and Whip Act, which directed that Quakers be tied to the
back of a cart and whipped as the cart slowly moved through the
town. When the cart reached the next town, that town would assume
the whipping duties until the procession reached the third town. This
routine would continue until the Quakers had been "whipped out" of
the colony. Though no longer an offense punishable by death, Quakerism remained a constant threat to non-Quaker colonists, who continued to respond with new manifestations of force.

The punishments for individuals convicted of practicing Quakerism in Massachusetts were similar to those mandated throughout
the colonies. Every New England colony except Rhode Island had
some form of anti-Quaker legislation on record in the seventeenth
century. Like Massachusetts, colonial New Haven imposed sanctions
against those who transported Quakers to Connecticut and those who
housed them in the colony, as well as against the Quakers themselves.
As in Massachusetts, New Haven leaders were most concerned about

repeat offenders. While they regularly banished Quakers visiting the colony for the first time, their punishments for returning Quakers were most severe. Their laws stipulated that:

> if after they have once suffered the law as before and shall presume to come into this jurisdiction again, every such male Quaker shall for the second offense be branded on the hand with the letter H, be committed to prison and kept to work till he can be sent away at his own charge; and for a third offense shall be branded on the other hand, committed to prison, and kept to work as aforesaid. And every woman Quaker that hath suffered the law there, and shall presume to come into this jurisdiction again, shall be severely whipped, committed to prison, and kept to work till she can be sent away at her own charge, and so also for her coming again she shall be alike used as aforesaid. And for every Quaker, he or she, that shall a fourth time herein again offend, they shall have their tongues bored through with a hot iron, committed to prison and kept at work till they be sent away at their own charge. And all and every Quaker arising from among ourselves shall be dealt with and suffer the like punishment as the law provides against foreign Quakers. (Vaughan 232)

The New Haven fear of Quakers "arising from among ourselves" was well-founded. Local conversions did occur, and the colonies enacted new laws to punish the new converts, though most of the local Quakers were treated less harshly than their visiting teachers. In *Neighbors, Friends, or Madmen,* a study of the growing accommodation of Quakerism in Massachusetts, Jonathan Chu argues that rather than any softening of attitudes toward the Quakers, the growing number of local conversions accounted for the increased toleration in Massachusetts in the late seventeenth century (153–54).

Quaker persecutions occurred less frequently in the southern colonies than in New England, but laws against Quaker activities there were no less severe. Virginia, for example, banished Quakers for their first offense and threatened them with death if they returned. In addition, magistrates in Virginia imprisoned both local and visiting Quakers and rescinded land claims of local converts (Lovejoy 120).

Maryland and New Netherlands both ignored the first Quakers within their borders, but attitudes there changed quickly. Soon after the first Quaker arrivals, John Yeo, an Anglican priest in Maryland, wrote to Canterbury that Maryland was becoming a "Sodom of uncleanness and a Pest house of Iniquity" because many of the colony's residents were turning to "Popery, Quakerisme or fanaticism." By the early 1660s Maryland had enacted stringent laws against the Quakers (Lovejoy 120–22). New Netherlands Governor Peter Stuyvesant, initially moderate in his attitudes toward Quakers, soon changed his position and banished all Quakers to Rhode Island immediately upon their arrival in his colony. His first victims were two young women who threatened the stability of his colony by preaching the Quaker truth in the streets (Lovejoy 120–21). Long Island, however, continued to be a gathering place for Quakers, who were allowed to live there relatively free of persecution.

Rhode Island alone had no anti-Quaker legislation, and as a result, the Quaker population there grew. Rhode Island's toleration, however, demonstrates less of a liberal attitude toward Quakerism and more of a practical solution to a growing colonial problem. Rhode Island recognized that the harsh punishments imposed on Quakers by Massachusetts and the other colonies failed to stop Quaker arrivals. That Massachusetts, the colony with the most severe anti-Quaker legislation, had the greatest influx of itinerant Quakers was evidence to Rhode Island officials that the Quakers, instead of running from persecutions, actively sought opportunities for martyrdom. Harsh and brutal punishments, they reasoned, would therefore attract rather than repel Quakers (Lovejoy 123). By failing to enact anti-Quaker laws, Rhode Island was not attempting to offer the Quakers a safe harbor. Instead, it was trying yet another solution to the growing Quaker problem.

As the geographic distribution of the anti-Quaker legislation and the severity of the punishments themselves indicate, the Quakers ignited fears deeply ingrained in early American culture. Attributing all of the Quaker persecutions to Puritan attitudes toward other religious groups, although certainly part of the story, offers too simple an explanation. To be sure, the Puritans' sense of themselves as a community of saints relying on a doctrine of election could not be reconciled with the Quakers' more democratic belief in the Inner Light. The Puritans limited salvation only to those people predestined before their birth to be counted among God's elect, while the Quakers believed that the potential for salvation was universal, and that one had only to turn inward to be saved.

The conflict between the Puritans and Quakers in early America, however, did not turn only on these theological disputes. Equally compelling were secular issues. The leaders of the seventeenth-century Massachusetts Bay Colony, already feeling the foundations of their theocracy trembling, considered the Quakers a threat to civic as well as sacred institutions. Charges against them in Massachusetts and throughout the colonies, often general in nature, place greater emphasis on their secular evils than their theological heresy. John Hull, a Boston merchant and local selectman, epitomized the common seventeenth-century objections to the Quakers when he wrote in his diary that he objected to these heretics because they were "persons uncivil in behavior, showing no respect to any, ready to censure and condemn all" (Chu 36). For Hull and his contemporaries, a Quaker's refusal to show deference to magistrates and ministers posed a social problem more immediate in Puritan daily life than any theological doctrine the Quaker might espouse. Most early colonists opposed to Quakers would have agreed with the London author of *The Character of a Quaker in his true and proper Colours; or, The Clownish Hypocrite Anatomized* (1671), who found the Quaker's most evident and obnoxious characteristic to be a contentious nature, leading to behavior contrary to common fashion:

> Should the Parliament make a Law *for Eating*, he would rather Starve than be *guilty* of obeying it, and if you would have him *do* a thing, you need only *forbid* it on pain of death; He thinks that to be *religious* one is obliged to be *uncivil*, and flings his Wits *overboard* to make room for *Inspirations*. (2)

Not all Quaker challenges to social mores in the colonies, however, were passive challenges caused merely by belligerence. Most of the early Quakers came to British North America as itinerant preachers, and their itinerancy alone raised the suspicions of colonists intent on establishing communal stability.[7] Mobility signaled vagrancy to the colonists, and Quaker itinerants often inadvertently confirmed the colonists' perception of them as agents of disorder. They had no qualms about entering Puritan church services, interrupting the minister's sermon with proclamations of the Quaker truth, and then charging the minister with being the Devil's mouthpiece. By failing to show the expected deference to the minister and by violating the Puritan practice of congregational silence in church, these itinerants transgressed both sacred and civic customs. Other Quaker preachers shocked the community by delivering their messages in the middle of the streets, often drawing large crowds. The rarity of street preaching in the early days of the colonies perhaps explains the reaction a Quaker woman received when preaching on a public street in New York. The Dutch settlers, understanding little English, assumed that the woman was sounding an alarm for a fire, and panic ensued until someone realized that she was a Quaker preacher and arrested her (Chu 38).

By the end of the seventeenth century, schisms developed among the Quakers, and more radical Quaker groups began to disrupt the more orthodox. One group, the "Singing Quakers," was excluded from the New England yearly meeting in 1697 for disturbing speakers by suddenly bursting into song during meeting. Sentinels posted at the door to the meetinghouse kept them from entering but not from gathering under the windows and periodically "singing" or intoning their disagreement with the speaker (Carroll, "Singing" 12). In her journal Sarah Kemble Knight described the Singing Quakers she met in Milford, Connecticut, as "humming and singing and groneing after their conjuring way" (112). In his attack on the Quakers, Roger Williams referred to this same group when he berated "their monstrous way of Singing and Toning and Humming many at once . . . when no man is edified, nor understands what they say" (Carroll, "Singing" 11).[8]

From passive resistance against social customs to overtly disruptive acts, the Quakers gave the seventeenth-century colonists reason for concern about their presence. By the eighteenth century, however, as the Quakers established communities of their own, they became a less formidable threat to the dominant colonial systems. Published attacks on them persisted, but their focus shifted from demonstrating that Quakers were agents of evil to showing that they were touched by madness. A small cast of characters from the early days of Quakerism in the colonies became stock figures in eighteenth-century anti-Quaker literature. Margaret Brewster, the last Quaker woman to be stripped and whipped in Massachusetts, became immortalized as a mad woman who entered Boston's South Church in 1677 dressed in sackcloth and ashes. Though not mentioning her by name, Samuel Sewall described the incident in his diary:

> In Sermon time there came in a female Quaker, in a Canvas Frock, her hair dishevelled and loose like a Periwigg, her face as black as ink, led by two other Quakers, and two other followed. It occasioned the greatest and most amazing uproar that I ever saw. (44)

Some eighteenth-century attacks on Quakerism specifically mention Brewster; others only allude to the mad woman in sackcloth and ashes. Nonetheless, the image of her entrance into the Boston church remains vivid in these accounts.

Deborah Wilson and Lydia Wardel also became major figures in the eighteenth-century anti-Quaker propaganda; as with Brewster, however, their actions are frequently only alluded to and their names not mentioned. According to accounts, Wilson walked naked through a Massachusetts town, and Wardel entered a Puritan church service naked. These incidents provide examples of the short-lived Quaker practice of "going naked as a sign" to onlookers that they too were naked if they had not experienced the Inner Light.[9] Even though this phenomenon occurred only during a twenty-year period in the mid-seventeenth century and has not been documented outside of Massachusetts, references to Quakers running naked through the colonies abound throughout anti-Quaker tracts in the eighteenth century as evidence of their madness. In the *Magnalia Christi Americana* (1702), Cotton Mather contributed to the popular image of the Quakers as mentally deranged by recounting the story of Mary Ross. Ross, a prominent Ranter in New York in the 1680s, belonged to a group calling itself the "New Quakers." According to Mather, Ross burned her clothes, referred to herself as Christ and to her two companions as Peter and Thomas, claimed that she had been dead for three days, and danced naked through the town after her "resurrection" (Lovejoy 142).

That the Quakers given prominent roles in anti-Quaker literature by eighteenth-century colonists are primarily women is no accident. Given the era's increasing religious pluralism, many Quaker peculiarities eventually ceased to be overt challenges to dominant cultural systems and became instead the tolerable, if still unsanctioned, ways of a peculiar people. Quaker practices that empowered women in the meeting by granting them equality in worship practices, however, remained more than a curiosity. The prominence of women within the Quaker meeting and the broader Quaker community continued to challenge the foundations of the patriarchal dominant culture in the eighteenth century, as it had in the early colonial period. With the Salem witchcraft crisis firmly embedded in their recent cultural memory, these later colonists had only to make a small leap to put women at the center of charges of Quaker madness.

    Though the brutal persecutions of Quakers had ceased by the eighteenth century, unfavorable images of them remained current and became part of the mythology informing anti-Quaker attitudes during Ashbridge's lifetime. The seventeenth-century image of Quakers as evil and the eighteenth-century image of them as mad both separated the Society of Friends from the dominant culture and reinforced their sense of themselves as "peculiar people." All of these attitudes contributed to the cultural baggage that Elizabeth Sullivan and her husband carried into the Wilmington tavern that night in 1736, and they fueled Mr. Sullivan's fears about Elizabeth's newly acquired Quakerism.

✳

In addition to the dangerous image of Quakers within the popular imagination, Mr. Sullivan had an even more pressing concern to face if his wife was a Quaker: she might become a preacher. Before leaving Pennsylvania Sullivan had become enraged when a church warden with anti-Quaker sentiments suggested to him that his wife would become a preacher. Ashbridge recounts that her husband, "in a Great rage," made menacing movements toward her and told her that she "had better be hanged in that Day" (161). The possibility of his wife speaking in public threatened Sullivan even more than did her Quakerism, for not only would she be a marginalized figure in society, but her role as a preacher would raise challenges to his entire existence by defying the accepted gender roles within their culture.

    Prohibitions and prejudices against women preachers surfaced throughout England and the colonies in the seventeenth and eighteenth centuries. In 1615, when Gervase Markham wrote about the need for the English housewife to be a religious guide for her family, he carefully guarded against being labeled an advocate for women in the ministry:

> I do not mean that herein she should utter forth that violence of spirit which many of our (vainly accounted pure) women do, drawing a contempt upon the ordinary ministry, and thinking nothing lawful but the fantasies of their own inventions, usurping to themselves a power of preaching and interpreting the holy word, to which they ought to be but hearers and believers, or at the most but modest persuaders; this is not the office either of good housewife or good woman. (6–7)

Samuel Johnson captured the prevailing sense that women in ministerial roles were unnatural oddities. According to his biographer, James Boswell, Johnson expressed the following opinion after hearing a female preacher:

> Sir, a woman preaching is like a dog's walking on its hinder legs! It is not done well; but you are amazed to find it done at all. (quoted in D. Johnson 326n13)

The pervasiveness of such attitudes is evident in the frequency with which Quaker women themselves mentioned their former dislike of female preachers. Margaret Lucas, one of Ashbridge's contemporaries, documented her reaction on first hearing a Quaker woman speak in meeting:

> The first time I ever heard a woman preach, from a prejudice imbibed from my companions, and, probably, from an aversion in my own nature, I thought it ridiculous; and the oftener I had opportunities to see it, the more I secretly despised it. At the time I joined with friends, this was one of my strongest objections to them; but I endeavored to silence it, by concluding, that others might do as they pleased and so would I. (96)

So strong was Lucas's aversion to women preachers that when God urged her to speak the Quaker truth so that others might know of her convictions, she resisted and developed a series of illnesses presumably caused by the stress of her resistance. In the height of her illness, Lucas vowed that her "choice was, rather to die, than live to be a preacher" (101). Another of Ashbridge's contemporaries, Jane Hoskens, received the call to speak at meeting and, like Lucas, resisted because of her attitudes toward women preaching. Hoskens's reluctance to preach was strengthened by her feelings of unworthiness for the task:

> I cryed in spirit, Lord I am weak and altogether incapable of such a task, I hope thou wilt spare me from such mortification, besides I have spoken much against womens appearing in that manner. (10)

To avoid disturbing "the quiet of others," she stayed away from Quaker meetings for long periods, avoiding the temptation to speak (12).

Elizabeth Ashbridge also describes her early attitudes toward women preachers. Long before her conversion, she heard a woman speak at a Boston meeting:

> I looked on her with Pity for her Ignorance (as I thought) & Contempt of her Practise, saying to my self, "I am sure you are a fool, for if ever I should turn Quaker, which will never be, I would not be a preacher."—In these and such like thoughts, I sat while She was Speaking; after she had done there Stood up a man, which I could better Bear. (155)

The speaker's gender more than the content of her message fueled Ashbridge's contempt. After becoming convinced of the truth of Quakerism, her initial reaction toward women preachers returned to plague her:

> Notwithstanding all my care the Neighbours that were not friends began to revile me, calling me Quaker, saying they supposed I intended to be a fool and turn Preacher; I then receiv'd the same censure that I (a little above a year before) had Passed on one of the handmaids of the Lord at Boston, & so weak was I, alas! I could not bear the reproach. (160)

Like Margaret Lucas and Jane Hoskens, Ashbridge at first went to great lengths to deny the possibility that she might become a preacher. Her frequent references to her own prejudices against women preachers suggest the power of the cultural pressures against this practice— pressures that formed part of the subtext underlying Mr. Sullivan's reactions to her Quakerism.

Women preachers posed problems in two different areas of eighteenth-century life. They violated both scriptural prohibitions and social norms governing early American culture. Doctrinal objections to women speaking in church found their basis in the Pauline injunctions against the practice, and opponents to the practice cited such passages as the following to support their stance:

> Let your women keep silence in the churches: for it is not permitted unto them to speak; but they are commanded to be under obedience, as also saith the law. And if they will learn any thing, let them ask their husbands at home: for it is a shame for women to speak in the church. (1 Cor. 14:34–35)

> Let the woman learn in silence with all subjection. But I suffer not a woman to teach, nor to usurp authority over the man, but to be in silence. (1 Tim. 2:11–12)

George Fox, founder of the Society of Friends, addressed these objections early in the group's history with a twofold defense of women ministers. First, he argued that Quakers could ignore Paul's prohibitions because the age of direct revelation was not over and the Inner Light could show new understandings of old teachings. Quakers, therefore, were not bound by old teachings that had been superseded by new revelations. Furthermore, he contended that the practice of women preaching had scriptural precedent: the scriptures contain numerous examples of women who spread the word of God, even though they did not preach in the usual sense of the word.[10]

Despite their currency in anti-Quaker literature, the doctrinal arguments against women preachers were probably not uppermost in Elizabeth Sullivan's mind nor in her husband's when the warden of the Anglican church suggested that she would become a Quaker preacher (161). More likely, the social implications of his prediction raised their anxieties.

The woman preacher filled a public role in the Quaker meetings and, if she traveled as an itinerant preacher, became known as a "Public Friend." With this public role came a certain degree of power and prestige—even in a Quaker meeting, which had several designated lay ministers yet permitted anyone to speak. Outside the meetinghouse, street preaching also gave women public visibility. The public role of the woman preacher, challenging the *feme covert* status of women in eighteenth-century life, effectively undercut the entire system of coverture, which provided legal and, implicitly, social restrictions on women's rights and property and subsumed them in their fathers' or husbands' lives (Salmon, "Equality" passim).

Quaker women preachers also faced opposition because their preaching frequently took them away from their families. Like the first Quaker preachers who entered the American colonies in the mid-seventeenth century, they were itinerants, and itinerancy still occasioned suspicion in the eighteenth century. Even the famous preachers of the Great Awakening—George Whitefield, Gilbert Tennent, and James Davenport—faced some of their strongest criticism because of their itinerancy, which was perceived as a source of instability within both the church and the community. Their opponents objected to the way they entered a town, incited people into a frenzy, and then left the local minister to deal with his congregation's emotional state. For women preachers, itinerancy was even more problematic in a culture emphasizing family stability as the basis for communal solidity. Popular perceptions associated itinerant women with the disruption of family life and the destruction of familial values. Patience Green became infamous as an illustration of this danger in anti-Quaker tracts. After an extended visit to the southern colonies to preach against slavery, Green returned to her home in Rhode Island to find one of her children dead and another dying. Despite this tragedy, she still felt compelled to leave home almost immediately to preach in England, Scotland, and Wales (Lovejoy 133). By transgressing the role of mother and wife and putting her ministerial career before her family, Green, like other female Quaker preachers, violated societal norms that dictated the home as women's first responsibility.

The image of the woman as preacher in early America is colored by the Puritan conception of the "good woman" and the "bad woman" —the former a helpmate and companion to her husband, the latter an independent agent subject to the devil's influence and powers. A wife and mother remained a "good woman" only so long as she performed her domestic duties and subordinated herself to her husband. Any deviance from this role generated suspicion (Ruether and Keller 132–33).

In this context, it is not surprising to find Quaker women preachers associated in the seventeenth- and eighteenth-century popular imagination with another version of the "bad woman"—the witch. The connection between women and witches dates back at least as far as the *Malleus Maleficarum*, a 1486 handbook for inquisitors in European witchcraft persecutions, which linked witchcraft with carnal lust, a trait the handbook states is insatiable in women. In an influential treatise of 1592, "A Discourse of the Damned Art of Witchcraft," English divine William Perkins revitalized this connection, asserting that "woman being the weaker sex is sooner entangled by the devil's illusions with this damnable art than the man." He summarized his argument with what he labeled an old Hebrew proverb: "The more women, the more witches" (Ruether and Keller 154).

The linking of Quaker women to witchcraft is most evident in a series of woodcuts and engravings of Quaker meetings depicting a woman preaching. Among the earliest paintings of the Quaker meeting is Dutch artist Egbert van Heemskerck's "Quaker Meeting," probably painted sometime in the 1660s. This painting spawned several engravings, etchings, and drawings, each slightly different from the original, many of them created by Quaker antagonists.[11] One consistent feature these paintings portray is a woman preaching while standing on an overturned wooden tub (fig. 1). While a tradition of "tub lectures" existed in the eighteenth century, this practice does not seem to have been prevalent among the Quakers.[12] If the tub appeared at all in Quaker meetings, it may have had more to do with providing a readily available platform for the speaker than with any theological tradition. In the latter sense the tub is important because in serving as the eighteenth-century equivalent of the soapbox, it emphasizes the public nature of the woman's role in the Quaker meeting, and thus highlights the threat these women posed to dominant societal norms, which relegated the woman to the private world of the home. Typically, these drawings depict the woman gesturing passionately, further emphasizing her prominence in the public sphere and also suggesting the fanaticism and excess enthusiasm attributed to the Quakers in the public imagination.

Another consistent iconographical feature in most of these drawings is the woman's costume, a version of the typical Quaker plain

Figure 1. Marcel Lauron's engraving of "The Quakers Meeting." (Courtesy of the British Museum, Department of Prints and Drawings)

style of clothing with either a white apron or a large white collar on a grey or black dress. Although this dress readily identified the speaker as a Quaker, her hat bears little similarity to the flatter, broader-brimmed hats worn by Quaker women (Gummere 189–228). The high-crowned hats depicted in these engravings are reminiscent of those popular among the lower and middle classes in mid-seventeenth-century England, where women wore "broad hats like the men, of beaver, with lower crowns, and caps beneath, tied at the chin" (Gummere 193). In the paintings and engravings, however, caricature rather than realism seems the likely goal. If the preacher in the tall black pointed hat suggests the stereotypic witch's hat, as at least one commentator has suggested (Gummere 194), the connection may not be accidental. Egbert van Heemskerck, the Dutch progenitor of the series of engravings, also had a reputation for painting spirited scenes of such countercultural groups as witches. A Dutch art historian characterized Heemskerck's paintings as depicting "wild, whimsical and uncommon subjects, as for example, the nocturnal meetings of witches, devils and ghosts, also drinking parties and rural merry-making"; and an English critic added wakes and Quaker meetings to the unusual scenes that the painter represented (Hull 18).[13] A plethora of imitations of Heemskerck's work, popular throughout the late seventeenth and early eighteenth centuries, perpetuated and exaggerated the caricatured image of the tub preacher. By implicitly and subtly suggesting similarity between those believed to be witches and Quaker women who, by preaching, also violated societal norms, this series of engravings demonstrates the association of evil with public women in the seventeenth- and eighteenth-century cultural imagination.[14]

❋

The societal fears surrounding the public woman did not first emerge with the formation of the Quaker meeting. They formed the center of an earlier 1637 controversy surrounding Anne Hutchinson, a woman whose story continues to surface throughout early American cultural history as the prototype of the female dissenter.[15] Hutchinson's story has particular relevance to the seventeenth- and eighteenth-century

attitudes toward Quaker women because of her relationship with
Mary Dyer.

The weekly gatherings that Hutchinson held in her home for
women unable to attend the church service began innocuously and
posed no initial threat to ministers or magistrates of the Massachusetts
Bay Colony. However, when these gatherings began to grow in size
and to include prominent colonial leaders, and when Hutchinson's
summary of the day's sermon evolved into commentary on the fitness
of the doctrine, she became a problem for sacred and secular leaders
alike. She claimed that all of the Boston ministers—except her theological shepherd, the Reverend John Cotton, and her brother-in-law,
the Reverend John Wheelwright—preached faulty doctrine. Undoubtedly these challenges would have threatened the church and the community even if they had been issued by a man, but, as the transcripts of
her trial indicate, her teachings caused particular problems because of
her gender. In his opening comments at the trial, Governor John
Winthrop explained that the meetings in Hutchinson's house had
been "condemned by the general assembly as a thing not tolerable nor
comely in the sight of God nor fitting for your sex" (Hall 312). By 1645
her fame had spread across the Atlantic. John Brinsley, an Anglican
minister in Yarmouth, England, used Hutchinson's story as the sole
warning of the dangers of female preachers for women in his own
congregation:

> Instance in that notorious Mastris Hutchinson of New-England,
> who under a colourable pretext of repeating of Sermons, held a
> weekly Exercise, whereby in a little time she had impoysoned a
> considerable part of that Plantation with most dangerous and
> detestable, desperate and damnable, Errors and Heresies. Hence-
> forth then no more Women Preachers. . . . (Ruether and Keller 189)

Female dissenters existed throughout early American history. Anne
Eaton, wife of Connecticut Governor Theophilus Eaton, for example,
shocked her community by challenging the practice of infant baptism
and walking out of a church service in protest (Dunn, "Saints" 587–88).
Yet the stories of most female dissenters are forgotten by later American culture, while Hutchinson's story remains prominent.[16] Hutchin-

son enters the cultural imagination of early America and, to a lesser extent, England as the symbol for the lone female dissenter in the colonies and as the prime illustration of the dangers associated with women preaching.

Hutchinson's association with women preachers in general would be enough to make her story relevant to an examination of the early American attitude toward Quaker women preachers, but her connection with Mary Dyer makes her story even more significant here. Dyer, an ardent Hutchinson follower before her conversion to Quakerism, attended Hutchinson's excommunication and reportedly rose and walked out of the church beside her banished friend. Even more portentous in light of the Puritan propensity to look for signs, both of these friends gave birth to deformed and stillborn children. In John Winthrop's account of Dyer's childbirth, he is careful to link Dyer with Hutchinson, an attendant at the birth. He implies that the shaking of the bed on which Dyer lay during this difficult delivery was a sign that the fetus itself was a devil, and that Dyer and her midwife were evil (Hall 280–81). To the early settlers of Puritan New England, these "monster births" confirmed beyond any doubt the disruptive nature of these two heretical women. These women violated their culturally prescribed roles as sources of stability within the home by becoming public figures, and they also provided evidence of their subversive natures by bearing monsters. Through her friendship with Dyer and through her early example of a woman preaching, Anne Hutchinson's story helps frame the attitudes toward Quaker preachers that persisted throughout the first centuries of American history.

The fears and frustrations of Mr. Sullivan in the Wilmington tavern in 1736 were thus constructed from a complex combination of collective memory and popular images informing the culture in which he lived. Memories of the brutal persecutions in the seventeenth century—kept alive in contemporary attacks on Quakers along with stories of their alleged madness and fanaticism—blended with the daily challenges Quakers posed to cultural norms governing acceptable behavior for women. These collective memories, along with the questions they raised about appropriate roles for women, continued to capture America's cultural imagination well into the nineteenth century.

Almost a century after the events in the tavern, Nathaniel

Hawthorne published "The Gentle Boy" (1832), in which he created
Catherine, a Quaker who embodies many of the characteristics popu-
larly associated with women preachers. Catherine, modeled in part
after Margaret Brewster, appears in a Puritan church "in a most singular array":

> A shapeless robe of sack-cloth was girded about her waist with a
> knotted cord; her raven hair fell down upon her shoulders, and its
> blackness was defiled by pale streaks of ashes, which she had strewn
> upon her head. Her eyebrows, dark and strongly defined, added to
> the deathly whiteness of a countenance, which, emaciated with
> want, and wild with enthusiasm and strange sorrows, retained no
> trace of earlier beauty. This figure stood gazing earnestly on the
> audience, and there was no sound, nor any movement, except a
> faint shuddering which every man observed in his neighbor, but
> was scarcely conscious of in himself. (81)[17]

Catherine not only acts in a way that could be read as the madness and
fanaticism associated with the Quakers, but through Hawthorne's
description she becomes both a "dark lady," with all of the implied
overtones of the temptress and the embodiment of sinister evil. She is
also akin to Hawthorne's Hester Prynne (*The Scarlet Letter* [1850]),
another dark lady more at home in the forest, the abode of witches
and the Black Man, than she is in the confines of the Puritan community. Hawthorne's Catherine bears some similarity to the "wicked"
women who practiced witchcraft.

Catherine also personifies the fear that Quaker women preachers
would destroy the strength of the family unit. When reunited with her
young son, whom she had believed to be dead, she tearfully embraces
him with a "joy that could find no words" (84), and yet moments later
decides that she must leave him to continue her preaching. The narrator interprets her tears as her recognition of "how far she had strayed
from duty in following the dictates of a wild fanaticism" (84). Like
Patience Green, the Rhode Island preacher who abandoned her dying
child to preach in Great Britain, Catherine chooses her public career
over what early American society would see as her primary responsibility—her family. She thus reinforces the image of the public woman
as evil. Catherine's oratory in the Puritan meetinghouse and her verbal

assault on the governor while imprisoned place her firmly within the
tradition of the disruptive public woman that had come to be associated with Anne Hutchinson, a connection that Hawthorne later
acknowledged in his depiction of Hester Prynne.

Hawthorne's characterization of Catherine can in many ways be
seen as the realization of Mr. Sullivan's worst fears as he tried to come
to terms with the possibility of being married to a Quaker preacher.
Although Sullivan would undoubtedly have failed to recognize
Catherine's romantic qualities of strength and power, he might other-
wise have seen her as a realistic portrait of the dangers and the problems associated with female preachers. Only in this context do Sullivan's actions in the Wilmington tavern begin to be understandable.
His inhumane and insensitive treatment of his wife are part of his
paternalistic sense of being able (and needing) to control his wife's
attitudes and beliefs. In so doing, he believed he would save her from a
life of persecution and prevent them both from existing on the edges
of eighteenth-century society.

Reconstructing this context is important not only in reading the
tavern scene, but also in understanding how Elizabeth Ashbridge, the
victim of abuse in the tavern and throughout her marriage to Sullivan,
ultimately comes to a sympathetic view of him in her narrative.
Although her narrative catalogs the persecutions heaped upon her by
her former husband, she suggests that she grew to care about him and
concludes her narrative with a tone of sorrow at his death:

> I never thought him the Worst of Men; He was one I Lov'd & had
> he let Religion have its Perfect work, I should have thought my Self
> Happy in the Lowest State of Life. (170)

Writing of these events from her retrospective view as an established
Quaker preacher fully recognizing the long tradition of Quaker persecutions throughout the colonies, Ashbridge could understand Sullivan's treatment of her. Although official sanctions against the Quakers
had lost their power, Ashbridge equates the personal domestic abuses
she suffered with the tests of faith sustained by the early Quaker martyrs who had endured legislated discrimination. As she narrates her
personal journey to the Quaker truth, these abuses become her badge
of honor that allows her to include herself in the hallowed roll of

martyrs. With this rationale, Ashbridge interprets Sullivan's abusive behavior as part of a long-standing cultural tradition and thus, in part, depersonalizes it. She realizes that he reacted against the cultural mythology surrounding Quaker women preachers rather than solely against her, even though she was clearly the focus of and occasion for his fears and anger. Because Ashbridge recognizes the power of the mythology surrounding her new role and the problems this role created for her second husband, she is able to put his actions into a broader cultural perspective and thus view Sullivan in a partially sympathetic light.

Not only is the popular image of the Quaker woman preacher important to a reading of Ashbridge's narrative, but it was also important to Ashbridge's composition of the narrative and to her means of making sense of her early life. Throughout her early years, if we are to believe her narrative, Elizabeth Sampson lived life on the margins of society. The tradition of the Quakers as peculiar people, set apart from the cultural mainstream, provided a way for Ashbridge to come to terms with this marginalization. It provided a link between her pre-Quaker experiences and her position as a prominent Quaker preacher —two extraordinarily different periods in her life that share little except a sense of being marginalized by the dominant culture. The cultural mythology surrounding the figure of the Quaker woman preacher became a useful narrative tool for Ashbridge the autobiographer, as she sought to make the story of her disparate lives into a unified whole. Because of her appropriation of this rich tradition, Anne Hutchinson, Mary Dyer, the women accused of witchcraft, and all of the early Quaker preachers stand in the shadows of her autobiography.

3

Power and Prestige as a Public Friend

Elizabeth Ashbridge's reputation as a prominent Quaker minister eventually extended to both sides of the Atlantic. In the early 1750s—almost twenty years after the Wilmington tavern incident—she visited England. When she and her traveling companion, Sarah Worral, accepted lodging at the home of Hannah and Samuel Corbyn of Worcester, the entire Corbyn household knew that they would be entertaining prominent visitors. Their American guests held important positions within the Quaker meeting, and their presence brought honor to the Corbyn home. Even Sarah Stephenson, Hannah Corbyn's young niece, sensed the importance of the visitors. Nonetheless, she could not have expected Ashbridge's visit to change the course of her life.

Stephenson, the eldest daughter of a prosperous English merchant, had been "introduced into company of high rank" as a young child. Even after her father overextended himself in business and was forced to separate his family because he could no longer support them, she continued to enjoy "a gentile stile" of life as a teenager in her Quaker uncle's home (Stephenson 13). Although she had frequent contact with Quakers, the life-style to which she had grown accustomed did not reflect the Quaker preference for plain style. Her taste for finery and the Quaker aesthetic of simplicity were poles apart.

One evening during Ashbridge's visit, Stephenson's attitude abruptly changed. Dressed in her usual attire, she conversed with the American visitors. When in the course of the conversation Ashbridge addressed the teenager "in the language of unspeakable love,"

Stephenson was completely taken with the woman and awed by her presence. As the evening ended and Stephenson was leaving the room, Ashbridge casually remarked to the Corbyns, "What a pity that child should have a ribbon on her head." To Stephenson, Ashbridge's "words were piercing," and they affected her so deeply that she lay awake all that night. The next morning, "not daring to put on [her] ribbon, [she] came down without it." Certain her family would notice the change, she feared that they would dismiss it as merely a young girl's theatrics, an attempt to gain favor with a distinguished guest, rather than as the first step toward "the gate of stripping" or the Quaker testimony of simplicity that advocated eliminating all superfluous ornaments. So great was her conflict, "both from within and without," that she "could scarcely contain" herself. Eventually Stephenson worked herself into a fevered sickness so severe "that it seemed not unlikely [she] might sink under it." During "this time of great weakness and reduction of will," she found the Inner Light, and recovered from her fever convinced of the truth of the Quaker teachings (Stephenson 15–16). Like Ashbridge, Stephenson eventually became a Quaker minister and traveled widely as a Public Friend.

✳

By 1753 Elizabeth Ashbridge had come a long way from her life as a persecuted new Quaker convert to the woman whose mere words could so completely change a young life. The powerful and lasting effect of Ashbridge's seemingly casual remark on Sarah Stephenson testifies to the esteem that the preacher then enjoyed within the Quaker community, for only the words of a highly prestigious figure would have had so dramatic an effect on her hearers. The Elizabeth Ashbridge of the 1750s, then a Quaker minister and autobiographer, was in many ways a different person from Elizabeth Sullivan, the early convert to Quakerism. The change in Ashbridge was much more than maturational. By the time she wrote her personal narrative, major upheavals had moved her from a life of persecution and marginaliza-tion to one of leadership and centrality within the Quaker community. Although the legal and social realities of the system of coverture still kept her in a subservient position as a woman, and the Quakers as a whole were still relegated to the margins of society,[1] within the Pennsylvania Quaker community Ashbridge had been empowered by her conversion, by her role within the Quaker meeting, and by her marriage to Aaron Ashbridge. No longer was she the new convert living outside the influence of the Quaker meeting and having to walk for miles to feel the security of a sense of community. Instead, her new life placed her at the heart of Quaker activity, and her success as a minister gave her prominence throughout the transatlantic Quaker community, as well as within Pennsylvania.

Ashbridge had gained visibility and a voice, and she had subverted the normal rules of the dominant society by placing her calling as a Quaker minister above her role as a subservient wife. Even though she chose to focus on her victimization when she told her life story in her personal narrative, she wrote from an empowered position and with a powerful voice. The narrative voice in her autobiography is one that young Elizabeth Sullivan lacked, but one that Elizabeth Ashbridge had gained along with her new status within the meeting and the community. No longer crying from the margins of the wilderness, this voice speaks from the heart of the community.

Ashbridge would claim that she had been led from the wilderness to the center of her community by the Inner Light of the Spirit. From the earliest days of her conversion, her Quaker faith empowered her, assuring her of the validity of her own beliefs and experiences—something that no other facet of her life had provided. Her Quakerism allowed her to accept her religious experiences as important and as genuine as any other's and to insist that she could discern the Truth as readily as could anyone else.

The central tenet of the Quaker faith—the only one clearly distinguishing the Quakers from their Puritan counterparts—is the belief in what later Quakers would term the Inner Light. While Puritans held that because one's salvation was ultimately a matter of speculation, one could never be certain of one's standing with God, Quakers believed that one could find assurance of one's salvation by turning inward. This Inner Light, rather than Scripture, became the final arbiter for Quakers, who denied that the age of revelation had ended. The same voice that spoke to the writers of the Scriptures, they argued, could also speak to each of them individually.

Inherent in the concept of the Inner Light was a belief in equality. For Quakers, the potential of each individual's inner spirit had a
democratizing influence. Quaker practices—such as their refusal to
take oaths, their refusal to remove their hats as an act of deference, and
their use of the familiar "thee" or "thou" instead of the polite "you" in
addressing people of all ranks—served as reminders of their belief in
equality. For Ashbridge and others like her who came to Quakerism
from a position of marginalization, this egalitarianism provided a new
sense of potency and worth. However limited this sense of power
might be in daily life outside the walls of the meetinghouse, converts
knew that at least in one segment of their life they could feel valued.

By giving her a more active awareness of contemporary politics,
Ashbridge's participation in the Quaker meeting also strengthened her
sense of self as an important member of society, for despite the Quakers' propensity for isolating themselves from the evils of the world,
they also took care not to sever themselves from their responsibilities
to the society in which they lived. William Penn, in his famous treatise
No Cross, No Crown, admonished his followers to "exempt not themselves from the conversation of the world, though they keep themselves from the evil of the world in their conversation" (Tolles, *Quakers*
75). Owing to this insistence on living in the world rather than withdrawing from it, issues of current importance frequently found a forum
for discussion within the Quaker business meeting. The issue of slavery, for example, was discussed in the Philadelphia Yearly Meeting as
early as 1696, when members officially discouraged the transporting of
slaves (Tolles, *Meeting House* 88n), as well as at the local meetings in
Chester and Goshen, Pennsylvania, beginning in the 1730s, when the
moral problems of slave ownership were recognized. Women who participated in the Quaker meeting had an unusual opportunity for public
debate on these issues.

Although Quakers in general escaped the fires of the Great
Awakening, this revival, which dominated religious conversation during Ashbridge's early days as a minister, became a major issue within
the Quaker community. Though she makes no mention of the revival
in her narrative, Ashbridge could not have avoided discussing this
phenomenon. Frederick B. Tolles suggests that the effects of the Great
Awakening were so prevalent in the middle colonies that "religion

replaced the weather for a season as the normal topic of conversation"
(*Quakers* 95). Benjamin Franklin observed that

> it seem'd as if all the World were growing Religious; so that one
> could not walk thro' the Town in an Evening without Hearing
> Psalms sung in different Families of every Street. (132)

Even the Quakers were preoccupied with the implications, if not the
fervor, of George Whitefield's visit to Pennsylvania and New Jersey.[2]
Whitefield, the English itinerant preacher who carried his evangelical
message to the American colonies in the 1740s, gained fame as the
most powerful Awakener ever to speak in America. Traveling from
town to town, he attracted huge crowds and inspired hundreds of followers. He visited Quaker as well as Congregational meetinghouses,
including the Burlington Meeting, where Ashbridge held membership
before her third marriage. John Smith, a member of the Burlington
Meeting, notes that on 23 June 1747 the meeting was particularly large
because "Whitefield, 2 Moravian preachers & several others that were
not friends were there" (Myers 98).[3]

   It must have been an extraordinarily empowering experience for
any woman living in eighteenth-century America to be an active and
valued participant in discussions about the theological and practical
problems of revivalism, the moral implications of slavery, and other
issues of current importance. Yet Ashbridge's role as a minister gave
her authority and influence even beyond that enjoyed by the majority
of Quaker women. She had occasion to speak before prominent
Quakers, as well as before renowned non-Quakers of George Whitefield's stature, and she had reason to believe that her audience would
listen. Catherine Phillips, Ashbridge's contemporary, provides evidence of how attentive the Quakers could be to the preachers. In her
personal narrative Phillips wrote that people often took notes while
she spoke (27). The Quaker meeting was thus a public forum that
empowered both the men and the women designated as its preachers.

   The honor and prestige accorded a Quaker minister was not easily won. Anyone present at a meeting could speak and theoretically
gain a captive audience, but in practice most of the praying and
preaching came from those designated and approved as lay ministers.
Being considered among the recognized ministers of a meeting meant

that one had spoken frequently in meeting and that the meeting deemed the speech to be good. In other words, the hearers were convinced that the prayers and the preaching resulted from the Holy Spirit working through the speaker and not merely from someone choosing to proclaim private feelings or ideas. The Quaker insistence on the unity of spirit within the meeting meant that only those revelations of the spirit relevant for all members were deemed appropriate utterances in meeting, and those who spoke in meeting were expected to appreciate the differences between appropriate and inappropriate occasions for speaking.

The emphasis Quakers placed on the appropriateness of the spoken word within the meeting can best be understood in relation to the value they placed on silence.[4] More than an absence of speech or other sound, silence symbolized attentiveness to the Spirit of God. In order to be attuned to the Spirit's voice within themselves, Quakers believed that they must suppress their self-will by eliminating worldly distractions and sitting quietly so that they might know the truth about their relationship to God.

The need for silence and quiet among Quakers also informed their daily routine in the workaday world. As Thomas Clarkson observed in 1808:

> The members, therefore, of the Society are expected to wait in silence, not only in their places of worship, but occasionally in their families, or in their private chambers, in the intervals of their daily occupations, that, in stillness of heart, and in freedom from the active contrivance of their own wills, they may acquire both directions and strength for the performance of their duties of life. (Brinton, *Friends* 135)

Consequently, one should not fill the silence with sounds—not even with the harmonious sounds of music. For, as Clarkson explains,

> Music, if it were encouraged by the Society, would be considered as depriving those of maturer years of hours of comfort which they now frequently enjoy in the service of religion. Retirement is considered by the Quakers as a Christian duty. . . . The Quakers, therefore, are of the opinion that, if instrumental music were admitted as

a gratification in leisure hours, it would take the place of many of these serious retirements and become very injurious to their interests and their character as Christians. (Brinton, *Friends* 135)

The emphasis on silence defined the Quaker meeting's essential characteristics for worship. Members of the meeting sat quietly until one of the adult members felt an "opening," or direction from the Spirit within them to speak. In theory, an entire meeting might pass with no one breaking the silence. In his autobiography, Benjamin Franklin described his first entrance into Philadelphia, when he unwittingly followed a crowd into a Quaker meetinghouse. He recalls the effect of Quaker silence on him, a weary young newcomer from Boston:

I sat down among them, and after looking round a while and hearing nothing said, being very drowzy thro' Labour and want of Rest the preceding Night, I fell fast asleep, and continu'd so till the Meeting broke up, when one was kind enough to rouse me. (29)

Just after her first glimpse of the Quaker truth, Elizabeth Ashbridge had an experience similar to Franklin's. She went to a meeting with her Pennsylvanian relatives and discovered to her surprise that the people sat in silence. Not yet understanding its importance in the Quaker religious practice, Ashbridge scornfully viewed the scene:

For as they sat in silence I looked over the Meeting, thinking within my Self, "how like fools these People sit, how much better would it be to stay at home & read the Bible or some good Book, than to come here and go to Sleep." For my Part I was very Sleepy & thought they were no better than my Self. Indeed at Length I fell a sleep and had like to fallen Down, but this was the last time I ever fell asleep in a Meeting, Tho' often Assaulted with it. (159)

Ashbridge's experience with the silent meeting for worship early in her convincement suggests the dilemma that the early Quakers faced by placing a premium on silence: can one silently bring others to a recognition of the Inner Light? (Bauman, "Speaking" 147ff). The Quaker minister's responsibilities included convincing non-Quakers of the Quaker truth, and this required breaking silence with speech. Yet speaking, like music and dancing, interrupted the silence that allowed one to be truly attentive to the Spirit of God. This predicament placed ministers in the uncomfortable position of knowing that in order to bring someone to the Quaker truth, they themselves must risk becoming less attuned to God. Because of the danger that speech would preclude the workings of the Spirit, Quakers wanted those who spoke to do so only when they were moved by the Spirit and when their message would strengthen the unity of spirit within the meeting. While it was important to speak only "in the light," the Quakers considered it equally important not to ignore a spiritual opening. One could be too hesitant about speaking as well as too forward. Finding the balance between avoiding inappropriate speech and wisely using every opening required extreme skill and an intimate knowledge of the workings of the Inner Light. Consequently, when a meeting found people like Elizabeth Ashbridge, who they determined possessed these abilities, they held them in high esteem and designated them as official ministers of the meeting. The delicate balance between speech and silence that Quaker ministers were expected to maintain helps explain the prestige attached to the role of the minister, and it also lends credence to descriptions in the ministers' personal narratives of the trauma they experienced when they felt their first opening in a meeting. For female ministers, cultural sanctions against women assuming public leadership roles compounded the spiritual pressures that they had to overcome the first time they spoke in a meeting.

The requirement that one speak only when moved to do so by the Spirit meant that good Quaker preaching was spontaneous. The Society of Friends' rejection of the traditional Protestant order of worship and its attendant formal discourse in favor of spontaneous testimony fundamentally signalled a peculiar set of assumptions about the nature of language and the primacy of extemporaneous speech. A speaker could not plan a prayer or a speech but instead had to be able to extemporize as the Spirit directed. Richard Bauman suggests that this emphasis on spontaneity accounts for the distinctive preaching style among the early Quakers, which was characterized by an "abrupt beginning, [a] lack of apparent organization . . . frequent pauses, and . . . great variability in the length of the utterances" ("Speaking" 150).

Although this rhetorical style prevailed during prayers and preaching within the Quaker meeting, in more public speeches outside of the meeting, the Quaker minister characteristically adopted a more forceful rhetoric capable of persuading even the most hostile critics of the validity of Quaker teachings (Bauman, "Speaking" 151). Thus, a minister who became a Public Friend and traveled in the ministry, as did Ashbridge, had to be a skillful rhetorician capable of adjusting her mode of delivery to fit the audience and the occasion. In addition, her education had to be broad and her faith firm, for, as Rufus Jones indicates, the goal of the Quaker meeting was to select a minister who was prepared rather than one who could prepare a sermon (xxvi). At the time she wrote her autobiography, Ashbridge's skills had earned her a firm position among a select group of Quakers known for their mastery of Quaker speech and silence.

Ashbridge was also moving in prominent circles. In contemporary documents her name is found among those of the most prominent Quakers, suggesting that her friends and acquaintances were influential within the community. John Smith, Pennsylvania assemblyman and Quaker, recorded in his diary his social contacts with other leading Pennsylvania Quakers, including frequent dinners with Israel Pemberton, patriarch of a wealthy Philadelphia family; Anthony Benezet, author; M. Yarnal and Jane Hoskens, eminent ministers; and Elizabeth and Aaron Ashbridge (Myers 88, 111, and passim). Elizabeth Ashbridge's signature, along with those of such notable Quakers as Smith, Benezet, John Woolman, and Pemberton, also appears on a 1752 letter from the General Spring Meeting of Ministers and Elders of Philadelphia to their counterparts in London.[5] The connection between prominent Quaker families and the Ashbridges is further revealed by a letter, written after Elizabeth's death, from Aaron Ashbridge to Pemberton, who is judged by one historian as one of the two "leading Philadelphia Quakers of the second quarter of the eighteenth century" (Tolles, *Meeting House* 121). In that letter, which accompanied "some memorials which [his] Dear Wife left in her own handwriting," Aaron asked that "when opportunity offers" his wife's papers "be sent to John Woolman at Mount Holly who hath requested the perusal therof."[6] In addition, Elizabeth's international travels in her ministry meant that her network of contacts spanned the Atlantic and that her abilities were recognized in Great Britain and Ireland, as well as in Pennsylvania, New Jersey, and throughout the Middle Colonies.

The official records of her home meeting in Goshen, Pennsylvania, further demonstrate Ashbridge's high standing. With such prominence, of course, came some friction. In 1751, for example, Hannah Eachus cast aspersions on Ashbridge's character. The meeting supported Ashbridge by disregarding the charges, issuing a complaint against Eachus, and, two months later, disowning Eachus (W. Ashbridge 50). Years later, upon receiving news of Ashbridge's death during her travel in the British Isles, the Goshen meeting issued a certificate commending her ability:

> [H]er conduct was orderly and becoming her Profession of Truth and her ministry very acceptable which is of good satisfaction to this meeting. (W. Ashbridge 50)

Even in England and Ireland Ashbridge was respected. By the time she arrived in Waterford "in the middle of the 12 mo 1755," recorded an Irish testimony to her, she was weak and in great pain, unable to travel easily to meetings. Yet despite these afflictions, her ministry there was successful. According to the Irish writer:

> Her mien and deportment in the exercise of her gift was comely and reverent, her manner of expression free from any affectation, clear and strongly ingaging. Above all, the overflowings of divine goodness accompanying, manifested she had been baptized into Christ who under these ingagements furnished her with a good degree of his heart Searching convincing power, the great and awful sense of it wherewith she was clothed was visible in her appearances and shewed that she had not lightly entered upon or ingag'd in that service, but was well qualified for it. . . .
>
> Her conversation was an ornament to the profession she made, tending much to edification, her memory strong, her judgment clear and penetrating, nervous in Arguement, of an Affable, chearful & amiable temper, even in times of great weakness. Affectation & stiffness were opposite to her yet as occasion required she was neither wanting or afraid to check that which tended to Evil, her Spirit humble tender & Simpathizing with the poor & afflicted &

had a word of Comfort unto Such as Occasion. (E. Ashbridge
175–76)

The National Meeting in Ireland, where Ashbridge died, compiled an
account of her final days and her last words to demonstrate that even
though she suffered great pain, she remained faithful to their ideal of a
successful minister. To this account, the Irish meeting appended the
following testimony as a tribute to Ashbridge:

> She was a woman of an excellent natural understanding: In conver-
> sation cheerful, yet Grave and Instructive. She felt the affliction of
> others with a tender sympathy and bore her own with patience and
> resignation. As a Minister, she was deep in Travail, clear in her
> openings; plain and pertinent in her expressions; solid and awful in
> her deportment, and attended with that Baptizing power which is
> the evidence of a living Ministry; and which so eminently attended
> her in the last Testimony she bore in a publick Meeting, in great
> bodily weakness, that most or all present were reached and deeply
> affected thereby; and a young woman was Convinced of the Truth,
> to which she bore testimony, as a seal to the finishing of her Service
> in the Work of the Ministry, in which being so owned of her Master,
> we have no doubt but she now receives the reward of the Faithful
> Servant and is entered into the joy of her Lord. (E. Ashbridge 174–75)

Ashbridge's autobiography also offers a measure of her achievement.
Eighteenth-century women were not encouraged to write autobiographies, and the fact that Ashbridge wrote hers suggests not only that
she, like most autobiographers, wanted to leave a personal memorial,
but also that members of her community considered her experiences
extraordinary and worthy of recording. As part of the genre of conversion narratives written by prominent Quaker ministers to spiritually
guide other Quakers, her narrative, like much of Quaker literature,
works from the example of the representative life. Although Quaker
writers valued speculative arguments about doctrine, they contended
that readers were more likely to respond to Quaker beliefs when they
encountered the force of the Inner Light at work in the experience of
another human being. In this regard, the first-person narrative of a
soul's conversion had extraordinary spiritual and rhetorical potential.
Yet, telling one's story in meeting was not quite the same as conveying

it in print. All Quaker writings, therefore, were brought before a committee appointed by the meeting, and only those deemed especially edifying or powerful were approved for publication (Frost 6). Not only was Ashbridge's narrative published, but owing to its popularity, it was also recopied and reprinted throughout the eighteenth and nineteenth centuries. Moreover, it is included in *The Friend's Library*, a mid-nineteenth-century collection of writings chosen by the editors as those most important for Quakers to know.

The Quakers with whom Ashbridge associated, the comments written about her both before and after her death, and her narrative all highlight the high status she had earned within the Quaker community. This position of prestige created for Ashbridge a life-style drastically different from the one she had endured as a young indentured servant and early convert to Quakerism. By the time she encountered young Sarah Stephenson, she had moved from a position of almost total powerlessness to one of considerable authority within her religious sphere. Her conversion and her activities within the meeting empowered her in ways she scarcely could have imagined when she first emigrated to the American colonies.

✳

Ashbridge's life-style, however, did not result solely from her prominence in the Quaker meeting. Her marriage to Aaron Ashbridge brought Elizabeth high social status and economic prosperity to which she was unaccustomed. She had been twice widowed by husbands who had not left her well provided for. Her second husband had left her deeply in debt, a debt that, as Aaron Ashbridge explained, she assumed even though by law she was not bound to do so:

> He left her near £80 in debt, for which by Law she was not Answerable, because without Effects; Yet as there were many Creditors who Complained, saying they would not have trusted him if it had not been for his Wife's Sake—she therefore (that truth might not Suffer) engaged to pay them all as fast as she Could; & as soon as Ability was Afforded settled to School keeping, whereby with her Needle she maintained her Self handsomely & by Degrees paid off near all the said Debts in the time of her widowhood. (E. Ashbridge 171)

With her third marriage in November 1746, however, Elizabeth moved into the kinship network of one of the most successful families in Pennsylvania. Having lived all her life preoccupied daily with economic survival, she suddenly found herself well-to-do. This transformation brought her both pleasures and problems.

The practical changes in her life were visible to her from her wedding day. Unlike her first marriage, when she eloped, or her second marriage, which she lamented as a form of bondage into which she entered for lack of other options, Elizabeth celebrated her marriage to Aaron Ashbridge. An 1842 account of old wedding customs in Quaker Philadelphia is suggestive of how elaborate her celebration may have been:

> The wedding entertainments of olden times were very expensive and harrowing to the wedded. The house of the parent would be filled with company to dine; the same company would stay to tea and to supper. For two days punch was dealt out in profusion. The gentlemen saw the groom on the first floor, and then ascended to the second floor, where they saw the bride; there every gentleman, even to one hundred in a day, kissed her. Even the plain Friends submitted to these things. I have known rich families which had 120 persons to dine—the same who had signed their certificate of marriage at the Monthly Meeting; these also partook of tea and supper. As they formally passed the Meeting twice, the same entertainment was repeated. Two days the male friends would call and take punch; and all would kiss the bride. Besides this the married pair for two weeks saw large tea parties at their home, having in attendance every night the groomsman and bridesmaids. . . . When these marriage entertainments were made, it was expected also, that punch, cakes and meats should be sent out very generally in the neighborhood even to those who were not visitors in the family. (W. Ashbridge 22)

Thus, when Aaron Ashbridge invited his friends to help him celebrate his marriage to his "sweetheart," we can suppose that the celebration was a joyous one:

> . . . My sweetheart as well as myself desire (if it may suit thy convenience and freedom), that thou wilt favor us with thy company at

our marriage, which is intended to be at Burlington the 4th of next
month.

> I am thy respectful friend,
> Aaron Ashbridge (W. Ashbridge 47)

The expense of the celebration would have been of little concern for
the Ashbridge family. Aaron's father, George Ashbridge, immigrated
to the American colonies in 1698 and immediately purchased seventy
acres of land in Edgmond Township of Chester County, Pennsylvania.
In 1708 he moved his family to Goshen Township, also in Chester
County, where he acquired a 341-acre tract of land. Gradually he
increased his property to 900 acres, one of the largest landholdings in
Pennsylvania (W. Ashbridge 3). Following in his father's footsteps,
Aaron also acquired substantial land, beginning with a farm deeded to
him by his father when Aaron was twenty-four years old on the occasion of his first marriage to Sarah Davies (W. Ashbridge 46).

The Ashbridge family's wealth gave them a natural opportunity
for leadership within their community, and family members assumed
active roles both within the Quaker meeting and within their community's political life. Names of first- and second-generation Ashbridges
appear throughout the records of the Goshen Meeting in the positions
of overseer, clerk, and elder. Aaron and his older brother, George,
served as officials in the civil government as well—Aaron as justice of
the peace and his brother as an assemblyman representing Chester
County in the Provincial Assembly (W. Ashbridge 31, 46–47). As
justice of the peace, Aaron assumed a position that brought with it
certain privileges and social standing outside of the Quaker meeting
as well as within it.

For Elizabeth Ashbridge, her newly acquired membership in a
family of means, as well as her role as the wife of a community official,
placed her in a position near the center of civic activity and near the
center of the community as a whole. For the first time in her adult life,
Ashbridge found herself away from the margins of society and near its
vital core. Although her Quaker faith kept her outside of society's
religious mainstream, she now had ample opportunity for important
interactions both within the meeting and the wider community of
Goshen. She had thus moved from indentured servant, constantly sat-

isfying the needs of someone else, to a woman whose own needs were of concern to others. Yet her new wealth and prestige did not afford her a life without problems. Her new position in society bumped up against her strong Quaker beliefs in ways that created new dilemmas for her.

The life-style of someone of Ashbridge's social status was at odds with her belief in the Quaker testimony of simplicity, and her new prominence forced her to define a golden mean that would accommodate both her religious and secular life. This problem was not Ashbridge's alone, but one faced by many Quakers whose economic successes in trade, industry, and real estate placed them in a class comparable in net worth to the wealthiest aristocratic southern planters. The conflict Ashbridge faced is inherent in the Quaker ethic that, on one hand, encouraged Quakers to be industrious and to view prosperity as a sign of God's blessing, while, on the other hand, cautioned them against excessive wealth. Wealth, they believed, would tempt them with luxuries and prompt them to violate their testimony of simplicity. The Quakers hoped that their emphasis on plainness would be a sign to the rest of the world of the dangers of greed and superfluity, and would consequently enable them to promote social equality and justice throughout the world (Shi 28–49). Quakers knew that being wealthy was not in itself evil, and they acknowledged the need to enjoy the fruits of their labor, yet they understood the temptations of greed and avarice associated with wealth. Wealthy Quakers needed to guard against the allure of luxury. For Ashbridge, who had lived most of her life as one of the economically disadvantaged, going without necessities as well as luxuries, these concerns and issues were new and perhaps heightened her sensitivity to such superfluous ornaments as the ribbon in young Sarah Stephenson's hair.

Despite the problems associated with her new life, Ashbridge had clearly moved into a realm of relative comfort. Aaron was able to care for her financial needs, she had established herself as a prominent figure in the Quaker meeting, and for the first time in her life, after two stormy marriages, she enjoyed the love and support of her husband.[7] She was as far away from her previous life on the margins of society as she could be while remaining a Quaker woman.

✷

Less than seven years after acquiring her new status in the community, Ashbridge suddenly gave it all up. She walked away from the physical and emotional comfort and security of her new home and went to England and Ireland to preach the Quaker truth, which to her provided an even stronger comfort and security. Like so many Public Friends who crossed the Atlantic in both directions during the late seventeenth and eighteenth centuries, Ashbridge so strongly felt the call to travel abroad in her ministry that it overpowered her feelings for anything that might keep her in Pennsylvania. In May 1753 Ashbridge joined the ranks of Quaker leaders taking their ministry to the other side of the transatlantic community of believers.[8]

Ashbridge did not write about her call to travel in her narrative, but several other Public Friends described their own decisions in detail. Each of them recounted an obsession with the idea of preaching abroad that could not be ignored. Elizabeth Webb's description of her "concern to travel" to the American colonies at the end of the seventeenth century is typical of the decision process delineated by these Public Friends:

> In the year 1697, in the sixth month, as I was sitting in the meeting
> in Gloucester, which was then the place of my abode, my mind was
> gathered into perfect stillness for some time, and my spirit was as if
> it had been carried away into America; and after it returned, my
> heart was as if it had been dissolved with the love of God, which
> flowed over the great ocean, and I was constrained to kneel down
> and pray for the seed of God in America. The concern never went
> out of my mind day nor night, until I went to travel there in the
> love of God, which is so universal that it reaches over sea and land.
> (Tolles, *Quakers* 26)

The call to travel created some difficult choices for these ministers. Traveling meant that they had to leave behind their family for long periods of time, since seldom were journeys abroad shorter than a year, and two- or three-year trips were common.

For Ashbridge the decision to leave her husband and home may have been made even more difficult by the short time she had known the strength of a supportive family. Aaron Ashbridge's lament over the loss of "a Darling and worthy Object, indeed of [his] Love & delight" supports this interpretation. He rationalizes his loss as a sacrifice to the "service of truth" and remains convinced that because his wife's "Lord & Master called her for Service abroad," she had no choice but to obey (E. Ashbridge 171). These, however, are only Aaron's words on Elizabeth's feelings about her journey. Entries in the Goshen Meeting records of the 1770s, some twenty years after Elizabeth's departure, raise the possibility that their marriage may have been somewhat less idyllic. After being "complained of" twice for drunkenness, Aaron was disowned by the meeting for excessive drinking, "so as to be disguised therewith on a public road" (W. Ashbridge 49). Had he been drinking while still married to Elizabeth, she would certainly have been re-minded of the misery that liquor brought to her marriage with Sul-livan, and these memories could have colored her attitude toward leaving Pennsylvania. Since Elizabeth does not write of her last years, we can only speculate about how she felt upon leaving her third hus-band. We do know, however, that once she felt "the concern to travel," she allowed nothing to stand in her way.

In addition to arranging their personal affairs and preparing for departure, itinerant ministers had to obtain permission from their home meeting to make the journey. The meeting typically appointed a committee to ascertain that the motivation for travel was genuinely inspired by the voice within and not merely a whim on the minister's part. Quakers considered a genuine calling a legitimate cause for leav-ing one's family, but frowned upon abandoning responsibilities in the home for frivolous reasons. On 19 February 1753 Ashbridge informed the Goshen Meeting that she "hath Drawings upon her mind to visit friends' meetings in Great Britain and Ireland," and they appointed a committee of three "to inquire concerning her conversation and min-istry." Less than one month later, a certificate was signed for her (W. Ashbridge 50), and she left Goshen and her husband to bring her message to the other side of the Atlantic.

Ashbridge and many like her traded lives of relative ease for an existence fraught with potential dangers. The voyage across the Atlantic was difficult at best; dozens of Quaker ministers chronicled the rough weather, seasickness, heat, and even shipwrecks that plagued their journeys. When they arrived in Europe, their discomfort often continued. Because they traveled great distances, most of these Public Friends were adept at horseback riding; yet, according to many narratives, poor road conditions often made their travel dangerous. Recorded mishaps include falling off or being thrown from their horses, scratches and scrapes from the trees and bushes growing over pathways, and becoming drenched and cold from fording deep and rapidly flowing rivers. When they stopped for a night's rest, they could never be certain what they would find. Not all Friends were as comfortably situated as were the Corbyns, through whom Ashbridge had first met Sarah Stephenson. Some nights were spent in inns that offered little more than a roof over their heads. Catherine Phillips, for example, reported lodging

> at a very poor lonely Scotch inn upon a chaff bed; our bed-room a ground floor, & no fastening to the door; & there being men in the house drinking, we were not quite easy with our situation. (42)

On other nights, Phillips would have welcomed even those amenities:

> Another night, we lay in the woods, with tolerable comfort, though the weather was cold, & the ground damp. About two hrs. before we stopped, as I was attempting to cross a swamp on some loose pieces of wood, one of them rolled, & threw me backward into it. One of our friends was leading me, & the other, seeing me in danger of falling, stepped behind me into the swamp, & caught me, so that I was wet but on one side, except my feet. (82)

Ashbridge's early years made her no stranger to such meager conditions, and she undoubtedly encountered many conditions like the ones Phillips described. However, her travel in Great Britain and Ireland also brought her to more congenial surroundings in the homes of wealthy Quakers. Since her reputation had preceded her, members of the host meeting often treated Ashbridge as an honored guest. Yet, even under the best of circumstances, her last years of life spent traveling abroad were arduous ones, and she sacrificed a great deal of physical comfort in her decision to leave her home in Goshen.

Ashbridge both gained and lost something by traveling. Her ministry in Ireland and Great Britain strengthened her reputation and influence within the transatlantic Quaker community, yet it also removed her from prominence in Pennsylvania as a member of the prosperous and influential Ashbridge family. Spiritually, that position had been a mixed blessing for her. Although it had given her comforts she had never before known, Quaker doctrine did not allow her to be content with them. She thus found herself having to measure her privileged life-style against the Quaker testimony of simplicity. Ironically, in Ashbridge's stormy marriage to Sullivan, a non-Quaker, she had had no wealth or prestige and, consequently, had been more easily able to follow the plain path of Quaker teachings. When she married into the staunchly Quaker Ashbridge family, however, her devotion to these principles was tested. In leaving Pennsylvania in 1753, Ashbridge may have found the best of both worlds. She removed herself from the temptations of wealth while still retaining the privileges that accompanied her spiritual position. She found time for the kind of silence that her faith demanded.

The dilemma of striking a balance between the different facets of her life and harmonizing them with each other lies at the heart of Ashbridge's personal narrative. Her narrative, focusing not on her achievement of prestige but on the period of her life in which she had nothing, attempts to reconcile these two very different conditions of her life. Coming to terms with the life changes she underwent was a difficult task, but her skill at balancing the realities of her existence with the ideal expressed in Quaker teachings allowed her to complete it. Her life experiences thus provided her with the solution to her complex narrative task.

4

Narrating a Life of "Uncommon Occurrences"

> My Life being attended with many uncommon Occurrences, some
> of which I through disobedience brought upon myself, and others I
> believe were for my Good, I therefore thought proper to make
> some remarks on the Dealings of Divine Goodness to me, and have
> often had cause with David to say, it was good for me that I have
> been afflicted &c. and most earnestly I desire that whosoever reads
> the following lines, may take warning and shun the Evils that I have
> thro' the deceitfulness of Satan been drawn into. (E. Ashbridge 147)

Eighteenth-century Quakers moved to write their spiritual autobiographies may never have had the experience of staring at a blank
sheet of paper, uncertain about how to begin, since they wrote within
an established genre providing formulaic opening phrases and predictable patterns of organization. Elizabeth Ashbridge begins her
autobiography in language provided by a long tradition of spiritual
writing. When she mentions the "uncommon Occurrences" attending
her life, she uses a stock opening phrase that suggests the singularity,
and therefore the importance, of the experiences that follow.[1] When
she attributes these occurrences to "the dealings of Divine Goodness,"
she follows the almost universal practice among Quaker writers of
viewing success as evidence of providential intervention in their lives.[2]
But by the end of this opening paragraph, she moves far beyond
generic commonplaces emphasizing exemplary piety and casts herself
as a woman who has suffered.

This opening paragraph signals Ashbridge's dual purpose. Knowing as she began her autobiography that it was to fulfill a spiritual purpose within the Quaker community, she also knew that composing the story of her spiritual journey would give her a chance to explain *to herself* the monumental changes she had experienced. Moreover, because opportunities for culturally sanctioned autobiographical acts were rare for eighteenth-century women, Ashbridge undoubtedly realized that this might be her only opportunity to make sense of her past and to tell about a life lived against the grain of the dominant culture.[3]

If the genre of spiritual autobiography provided Ashbridge with an invitation to tell her life story, it also put constraints on the telling. As Luella Wright has argued in her classic study of Quaker writing, "the Quaker autobiographer was a Friend first, and an individual penning his memoirs second," and voluntary consent to these priorities gives Quaker personal narratives their special flavor of a group voice speaking through the individual (156).

Ashbridge's narrative, like those of her contemporaries, follows the standard practice of describing childhood, marriage, all the details of convincement, and the attempts at altering one's life to fit a regenerate state. After her opening statement of purpose, she narrates events of her youth and her early search for a religious community where she could feel at home, and she briefly mentions her first two marriages. She also includes the requisite account of her convincement and spiritual torment surrounding that event. In the narration of her stormy life with her second husband, Quaker readers could readily find graphic evidence demonstrating Ashbridge's daily efforts to live in accordance with her new beliefs.

Yet, despite its conformity to the basic generic plot, Ashbridge's narrative is filled with details of her personal life. In this regard it differs significantly from those of her contemporaries. Three historians have independently concluded that Quaker writers seldom included details from their private world that did not have direct and obvious relevance to their religious lives. Howard Brinton finds "very little material about the writers' families and undertakings not directly related to their inner life" (*Quaker Journals* vii); J. William Frost notes that these narratives contain "almost no details of actual living" (31); and Luella Wright explains that the Quaker narrator treated "occurrences of life a little out of the ordinary . . . with extreme caution; moreover he is apt to exclude all such episodes" entirely (188). Elizabeth Ashbridge ignored these conventions; she seized on events more than "a little out of the ordinary" and made them the centerpiece of her personal narrative.

While her narrative reflects the genre's public function, it stands apart in that the communal voice is neither the first nor the only one we hear. Ashbridge combines a heavy dose of the personal with the public function of her narrative precisely because her story is so re-markable. When she says she writes because her life is "attended with many uncommon Occurrences," she participates, to be sure, in the broader tradition of labeling experiences uncommon and therefore worthy of attention. In Ashbridge's case, however, this stock phrase is not empty. Her life is a seemingly endless series of "uncommon Oc-currences" and "Remarkable Experiences," both in the sense of being noteworthy and in the sense of being truly extraordinary. In her posi-tion as an established Quaker minister, she had daily reminders of the enormous changes she had undergone from her early years of suffer-ing, and the autobiographical act gave her the chance to explore the meaning of those changes.

How as a Public Friend could Ashbridge write a narrative that included the disparate periods in her life? How could she make her spiritual journey appear exceptional enough to be worthy of emulation, yet typical enough to make emulation possible? Because she could never completely submerge her individual voice in the communal voice as she sought meaning in her "uncommon Occurrences," we hear two voices in her narrative. The struggle between the personal and the public voice gives Ashbridge's autobiography its special energy and interest as literature. By maintaining a strong sense of her story as extraordinary and uncommon, she wrote a narrative that is itself extra-ordinary and uncommon, fulfilling the basic requirements of a Quaker spiritual autobiography while stretching the genre's limits. In relating her "Remarkable Experiences," Elizabeth Ashbridge becomes an auto-biographer as well as a spokesperson for Quaker piety.

✳

In writing a document that both served a purpose in the public Quaker community and fulfilled personal aims, Ashbridge had to bor-row from the skills of historians and novelists alike. Like a historian, she cared about *what* had happened and *when* it occurred. Authenticity or believability required that she get her story "right" by recreating as closely as possible the world in which she had lived. Unlike the historian, however, she did not follow a paper trail to document her story but used memory and lived experience as her primary evidence. As Paul Murray Kendall demonstrates in his classic study of biography, the use of memory is what distinguishes autobiography from history and biography:

> Autobiography is not the true picture of a life; it is a true picture of what, at one moment of the life, the subject wishes, and is impelled, to reveal of that life. (Kendall 30)

The autobiographer must create a world from recollection that fits with how she imagines the past must have been in order for her life to have turned out as it did. Authenticity for the autobiographer, then, involves more than being true to the facts. Ashbridge had to make her story true to what she believed to be the ultimate reality of her life.

Current theories of autobiography show how creation of the self in the personal narrative brings the autobiographer into the realm of the novelist. Since in creating the self, the autobiographer's only access to the past is through present memory of it, the self depicted by the autobiographer is more a function of recollection and imagination than it is a representation of past reality. Evidence now suggests that often people "imagine part of what they believe they remember" and that they are sometimes "unable to distinguish . . . between memory and imagination" (Spacks, *Imagining* 19). The self that emerges in autobiography, therefore, is essentially a fictive creation, and "autobiographical truth is not a fixed but an evolving content in an intricate process of self-discovery and self-creation" (Eakin 3).[4]

Recognizing the autobiographical self as a fictional character, however, should not suggest that it bears no relation to the life lived. As Janet Varner Gunn argues, the autobiographical act is deeply embedded in the *culture* of the autobiographer.[5] "When the autobiographer brings a life 'to language,' he or she always adumbrates a perspective from somewhere—namely from a world whose meanings and codes . . . serve to locate and ground that perspective" (Gunn 9). Based on her study of eighteenth-century narratives, Patricia Meyer Spacks supports this view, asserting "the inadequacy of any understanding of self and its presentations that fails to consider also the fact of society and its shaping force on identity and identity's documentation" (*Imagining* 90). Autobiography, then, is an interpretive act, the "cultural act of a self-reading" (Gunn 8), that seeks to place the created self in a cultural context. From this theoretical perspective, "Where do I belong?" becomes the central question for the autobiographer, and "the question of the self's identity becomes a question of the self's location in the world" (Gunn 23).

For a spiritual autobiographer, placing the self in a cultural context poses less of a problem than it does for other personal narrators, because the genre of spiritual autobiography locates the narrative and the narrator within a spiritual, and usually a denominational, tradition. Hence, the genre makes some of the narrative choices easier; as Spacks notes, "spiritual autobiography as a literary form provides obvious securities for author and reader alike" (*Imagining* 28). The Puritan or Quaker autobiographer, for example, grounds the self through the act of writing within a specific community of believers. Moreover, the spiritual autobiographer must define identity in terms of an individual relationship with God and can present changes in character in ways predicted by the genre. Spiritual autobiographies written by eighteenth-century women exemplify the shaping influence of the preset genre. These narrators learned what story to tell from "cultural practices that confined their subjectivity, and from religious doctrines that forced closure on their ideas about identity and selfhood" (Nussbaum, "Commonplaces" 151). Consequently, many critics have undervalued spiritual autobiographies, dismissing them as mere formula. However, as Ashbridge's narrative demonstrates, spiritual autobiographers may play fast and loose with the formula, writing almost simultaneously both within and without the tradition. While the genre may prescribe certain patterns of self-creation, the autobiographical self that emerges may have more complexity than generic conventions can accommodate.

Spiritual autobiography privileges certain kinds of experiences, giving greater significance to those that identify and define the narrator's religious life than to those that reflect secular existence. Authenticity in a spiritual autobiography has as much to do with the correspondences between the narrated spiritual experiences and the spiritual norms of the tradition in which the author writes as it does with the degree to which those experiences ring true to the narrator's particular life. Just as seventeenth-century Puritan congregations judged the truth of spiritual narratives presented by candidates for full membership in the church, the religious community for whom the spiritual autobiographer writes is empowered to decide which autobiographies are authentic. Those deemed useful in the Quaker community, for example, were printed by Quaker publishers and circulated among the members of the meeting. Throughout the seventeenth and eighteenth centuries, spiritual autobiographies were by definition a communal activity.

The role of the community becomes even more apparent in a specific type of spiritual autobiography: the conversion narrative. The main purpose of a conversion narrative is to document the autobiographer's sense of belonging to a particular community. In Puritan versions faithfulness to the standardized conversion process became a criterion by which the community judged the validity of the experience. The successful Puritan conversion narratives describe the experiences of "conviction," or knowledge of sin, usually gained through attendance on the Word and knowledge of the Law; "compunction," or fear of punishment for sinfulness; and "humiliation," a recognition of their narrators' totally unregenerate condition in which they acknowledge that total reliance on God is the only hope for salvation. Following this recognition, the Puritans catalog their attempts to live uprightly and their inevitable backslidings into sinfulness.[6] Although at first glance Quaker conversion narratives appear less standardized, they in fact follow an equally predictable plot. Beginning with a statement of purpose, similar to the one in the opening paragraph of Ashbridge's text, Quaker narrators typically provide only a brief description of childhood, early religious crises, and marriage, and then offer greater details about their conversion (Wright 166). Their conversion process generally includes a long period of personal conflict and searching for religious truth during adolescence, followed first by "convincement"— a specific event during which the authors come to know the truth of Quaker teachings—and then by conversion, which is not a single event but a daily process of aligning their lives with their new convictions. Where Puritans see scripture and preaching initiating the conversion process, Quakers emphasize a more immediate experience of the Spirit coming only through silence. While both Puritan and Quaker narrators catalog prolonged struggles between sinfulness and God's will, the Quaker narratives often include dreams or visions dramatizing the opposing forces of God and Satan. For both the Puritans and Quakers, conversion led ultimately to assurance, insofar as they could achieve it in their lives. For the Puritans, assurance meant that the narrators were "elect," souls chosen by God to enter into the Covenant of Grace with Him, and, therefore, among the elite within the Puritan community. For the Quakers, the conversion narratives document the souls' recognition of the truth that dwells within everyone and their newfound ability to discern that Quaker truth.

These widely accepted and firmly fixed conventions of Quaker conversion narratives, evident from the early days of Quakerism in seventeenth-century England, were perpetuated by the requirement that, before being published, all Quaker writing needed the approval of the meeting. It is hardly surprising, therefore, that Quaker autobiographies strongly resemble one another. (Yet one should not conclude that Quaker authors wrote under coercion; Luella Wright argues to the contrary that Quaker autobiographers, recognizing the public function of their personal narratives, submitted voluntarily to the group sanction [158].)

Because Quakers believed that everyone could find the Inner Light, their conversion narratives were designed less to test the authenticity of their own spiritual experiences than to serve several other purposes. Ministers documented their exemplary piety in the hope of guiding others and supplying them with models for emulation. The narratives also served an archival purpose for the Quaker meeting. By circulating and publishing them, the meeting preserved for posterity the lives of its saintly members. Other writers had more practical uses in mind. As Quaker historian J. William Frost has noted, the hagiographic quality of these texts made them readily available preaching tools (31). These documents added to the Quaker arsenal of defense by providing excellent rebuttals to attacks on Quaker doctrine and the Quaker way of life. Beneath these exemplary, preservationist, and practical motives lay intense psychological needs. The particular practices of the Quaker faith made the kind of self-expression found in the journals and spiritual autobiographies inevitable. Quakers' doctrinally obsessive concern with the Inner Light gave them the introspective cast of mind that leads logically to autobiographical expression (Wright 194).

Ashbridge most certainly shared with her Friends a concern with the doctrine of the Inner Light and the introspective mindset that placed her narrative within both the general tradition of Quaker spiritual autobiography and the more specific genre of the Quaker conversion narrative. At the core of her autobiography is her conversion. Yet we see little of Elizabeth Ashbridge, Public Friend, in the text. Unlike her contemporaries who devote most of their text to tales of preaching and traveling, Ashbridge focuses primarily on her life before she gained prominence. In doing so, she positions herself both inside and outside the tradition. The struggle to create herself as a character would have been easier had she depicted herself only in the role of successful minister, a model of achievement that would comfortably fit her new life as a Quaker. But this characterization would have failed to account for the widow, the exile, the immigrant, the kidnapping victim, the servant, and the abused wife. Ashbridge needed to find a way to account for all the roles that she had played, for she could achieve authenticity only with a self-portrait that rang true to her own sense of all parts of her life. When she turned to autobiography, her private search for meaning would not allow her to grasp the easy narrative solution of adopting a voice that ignored the early part of her life.

In choosing to tell all the details of her early life, rather than just those of her conversion, Ashbridge gives her narrative a multivocality that transgresses the generic limits of spiritual autobiography. Multiple cultural codes inform her narrative, and the self that she constructs is layered. Her protagonist reflects not only the Quaker tradition in which she wrote but also her familial relations, her experience of immigration, her early economic marginalization, and the cultural realities of being a woman in eighteenth-century British North America. Her text shows a complex combination of the genre's formulaic requirements, her bizarre life experiences, and the unusual narrative decisions made in the process of self-creation. As a spiritual autobiographer, Ashbridge writes in the tradition of Jonathan Edwards and

John Woolman, her contemporaries; but as a woman telling her life story, she shares more with Anne Bradstreet, who implicitly questioned the Puritan system even as she lived and wrote within it. Firm in her Quaker convictions, Ashbridge struggles with the broader questions of how her life—before and after her conversion—fits into a broader cultural or spiritual scheme. Like all autobiographers, she asks "Who am I?" and then wrestles with an answer. More poignantly, she asks "Where do I belong?" This question speaks volumes when uttered by a voice on the margins of the dominant culture.

✳

Most eighteenth-century Quakers wrote their conversion narratives with a sense of wholeness, a feeling of communion with the Society of Friends, and a connectedness to the world. Elizabeth Ashbridge did not. Although she shares with her contemporaries the view of a disconnected pre-Quaker life filled with discontent, her conversion does not conquer all of the impediments in her life. Instead, she recounts an unending series of pre- and postconversion trials, abuses, and adventures that separated her from the connections she wanted. All her life, Ashbridge tells us, she sought attachments, and throughout her life these efforts failed. Despite continued attempts to find a sense of community, she finds only a pattern of isolation and alienation, themes that are not foreign to Quaker autobiographies since separation was an expected step on the path toward the Quaker truth. Quaker writers frequently tell of breaking away from one community so that they can emerge after their conversion as part of their new religious community. Ashbridge, however, carries these themes far beyond the genre's formulaic expression, making them the filter through which she sees all of her experiences and the design through which she presents her story.

When Ashbridge searched for events with which to characterize herself, she remembered primarily incidents involving separation and alienation. Choosing to recount them, she emphasizes the tension between her need to belong, or to be "at home," and the wrenching disruption that she felt. An impetuous decision launched her alienation. Admiring both her father "that bore a good Character" and her mother "who was a pattern of Virtue" (147), she nonetheless acted counter to their wishes, eloping with a stocking weaver at age fourteen and thereby separating herself from the family network she desired. Soon after this "precipitate action," she was "smote with remorse" over her disobedience to her parents and knew that she should have heeded their guidance (148).[7] The second major separation of her young life— her husband's untimely death after only five months of marriage—left her disconsolate. Widowed and alone, she had "no home to fly to" because her "Father was so displeased, he would do nothing" to help her, and she was forced to live with relatives in Ireland "in hopes that Absence would regain [her] Father's Affection" (148).[8]

Ashbridge responded to this breach by reasserting her will and her independence in a radical way: she fled the country and emigrated to the colonies:

> My father still keeping me at such a distance that I thought myself quite shut out of his Affections, I therefore Concluded since my Absence was so Agreeable, he should have it. (150)

Ashbridge describes her move to the colonies in the language of separation. It was a move *away from* her home rather than *toward* any new excitement or opportunity, and it served to increase the distance and enforce the alienation that she felt from her father.

Ashbridge portrays herself during these teenaged years as spunky, impetuous, and sometimes petulant, yet her spiritedness and independence never completely mask her desire to return home. The depiction of these early years establishes the character that gradually emerges in the narrative. The protagonist evolves into a strong-minded, independent woman who rebounds from horrific abuses. Still, despite this resilience, she is constantly alone and alienated. Without her family, she feels unconnected and detached. Her quest for a sense of belonging and attachment, for a surrogate "home," dominates the narrative. While Quaker conversion narratives frequently use the metaphor of a search or a journey to describe the process of coming to Quakerism, Ashbridge's journey is not only religious. As a Public Friend, she documents her spiritual journey and its fulfillment, but as an autobiographer seeking to rationalize the details of her life, she writes of her journey toward a sense of wholeness that could come only with a personal sense of belonging. Her narrative documents her literal search for what William A. Clebsch has called a state of "being at home in the universe" (xvi).

In serving its public function as a conversion narrative, Ashbridge's text documents a spiritual journey that takes her from one religious group to another in search of a comfortable spiritual home. Raised in the Church of England, young Elizabeth felt cut off from her church as well as from her family; yet, the Quaker narrator remembers her early fascination with religion:

> In my very Infancy, I had an awful regard for religion & a great love for religious people, particularly the Ministers, and sometimes wept with Sorrow, that I was not a boy that I might have been one; believing them all Good Men & so beloved of God. . . .
>
> As I grew up, I took notice there were several different religious societies, wherefore I often went alone and wept; with desires that I might be directed to the right. (148)

While her lament at not being a boy obviously foreshadows the comfort she finds in awakening to the Quaker truth and the Friends' acceptance of women preachers, Ashbridge's early interest in the variety of Christian denominations also prefigures her spiritual journey.

For Ashbridge, the search for a new religious home began almost immediately after losing the security of her parental home and being exiled to Ireland. Having "contracted an intimate Acquaintance with a Widow & her Daughter that were Papists" (149), Elizabeth was drawn to Catholicism, a liturgical tradition not unlike the Anglican one in which she had been raised. After investigating the tenets of the Catholic Church with an intensity and a sophistication unusual for such a young woman, she rejected this potential home because of the Catholic belief that "whosoever died out of the Pale of that Church was damned" (149). Thinking of her own "religious Mother who was not of that opinion" (150), young Elizabeth felt the pull of her familial ties more strongly than those of the church and decided to continue her quest.

The search for a spiritual home becomes a stronger theme in Ashbridge's narrative when she recounts her arrival in the colonies and her marriage to Mr. Sullivan. Deeming Sullivan's propensity to "ramble" disagreeable, and knowing that constant mobility could only increase her sense of disconnectedness, Elizabeth seized on their geographic relocation as an occasion to experiment with different religions. Traveling gave her the opportunity to meet with different congregations. More important, Ashbridge's unhappiness with Sullivan— "a man [she] had no Love for & that was a Pattern of no good to [her]" (154)—forced her to look outside their home for fulfillment. As a means of self-preservation in the face of intense despair, Elizabeth resolved to express her love for God more actively and once again to concentrate on her duty toward Him. Ironically, her resolve also improved her marriage:

> To Set my Affections upon the Divine being & not Love my husband seemed Impossible: therefore I Daily Desired with Tears that my Affections might be in a right manner set upon my husband, and can say in a little time my Love was Sincere to him. (154)

Yet, even with this new attitude toward Mr. Sullivan, the marriage still lacked the sense of belonging and contentment that she wanted. She thus continued her search for community.

After conversing with the neighborhood Baptists, Elizabeth became convinced that belief must come before baptism, and she grew uneasy about her own infant baptism in the Anglican church:

> At Length thinking it my Real Duty, I was In the Winter time Baptised by one of their Teachers, but Did not joyn Strictly with them, tho' I began to think the Seventh Day was the true Sabbath, & for some time kept it. (154)

Still her search did not end. While traveling in Boston, Elizabeth conversed

> with People of all societies as Opportunity offer'd & like many others had got a Pretty Deal of Head Knowledge, & Several Societies thought [her] of their Opinions severally; But [she] joyned Strictly with none, resolving never to leave Searching till [she] had found the truth. (155)

In Boston Elizabeth also attended a Quaker meeting, "not expecting to find what [she] wanted, but out of Curiosity;" she thus remained "a

Stranger to the Cause" (155). When her husband was hired as a school-master in Rhode Island, Elizabeth became acquainted with "the most Religious" of the local Presbyterians and found herself attracted to their principles. In her retrospective autobiography, Ashbridge inter-prets this attraction as indicating her continuing dissatisfaction and demonstrating that "the old Enemy of [her] Happiness" was still at work within her (155). After moving once again, Elizabeth found her-self near an Anglican church, the church of her childhood: "Tho' [she] Disliked some of their ways, yet [she] liked them best" (156). Feeling like a stranger and in the throes of despair, "bemoaning her Miserable Condition," Elizabeth felt that she had to join with some church and, because it seemed "nearest," she chose the Church of England (157). She immediately felt "released from Deep Distress," "content," and willing to "Submit to . . . Providence" (158). Finding security in the familiar, she believed the best spiritual home would evoke the family home she had lost.

But her contentment proved temporary. Shortly after her reaffili-ation with the Anglican Church, she "Got Leave of [her] Husband" to visit relatives in Pennsylvania, and, during the visit, found the ultimate truth in Quaker teachings. Her first recognition of it was a private one centering around her emotional reaction to reading an epistolary book that she had found at her uncle's house by the Quaker Samuel Crisp:

> [I] had not read two Pages before my very heart burned within me and Tears Issued from my Eyes, which I was Afraid would be seen; therefore with the Book (Saml. Crisp's Two Letters) I walked into the garden, sat Down, and the piece being Small, read it through before I went in; but Some Times was forced to Stop to Vent my Tears, my heart as it were uttering these involuntary Expressions; "my God must I (if ever I come to the true knowledge of thy Truth) be of this man's Opinion, who has sought thee as I have done & join with these People that a few hours ago I preferred the Papists before?" (158–59)

In keeping with the pattern established throughout her early years of feeling isolated and alone, unable to trust anyone, Elizabeth experi-enced this emotion in private. Yet she came to perceive the truth and to begin her affiliation with the group that would ultimately lead her to prominence and security not when she was completely alone and isolated, but rather when she was in the fold of a family for the first time in the years since she left England. Her discovery of religious community came with her renewal of familial ties, a coincidence not lost on the narrator. In recounting her initial encounters with Quakerism, Ashbridge stresses not a commitment to the Quaker faith but a desire to join with people as the motivation for what she describes as an almost serendipitous attendance at the Quaker meeting in Pennsylvania:

> The next Day being the first of the week I wanted to have gone to Church, which was Distant about four Miles, but being a Stranger and having nobody to go along with me, was forced to Give it out, & as most of the Family was going to Meeting, I went with them, but with a resolution not to like them. (159)

Even after her powerful emotional, though private, encounter with the power of the Quaker teachings, Elizabeth's first public encounter with a Quaker meeting was less than auspicious. In a manner similar to what Benjamin Franklin described some years later in his autobiography, she "fell a sleep, and had like to fallen Down" because of the silence she encountered (159).[9] Shortly after this meeting, however, Elizabeth realized that the Quakers were the people with whom she must join. Within the Quaker meeting she knew that she would find the community and the sense of belonging that she had lacked since she left her family many years earlier.

In most Quaker conversion narratives, the end of the search is the high point—the instant when one recognizes the power of the Inner Light and the rightness of the decision to join with the Quakers. At this juncture, Ashbridge's contemporaries typically begin to record major events in their preaching careers, beginning with the usually emotionally wrought experience of speaking for the first time in their home meetings. These narrators then undertake a detailed accounting of meetings they have attended, occasions on which they have spoken, communities that they have visited, and other Quaker preachers whom they have heard speak or with whom they have traveled.

Ashbridge's narrative follows none of these conventions. At the point in her text where she finally finds the Inner Light and community—the point at which readers might expect her to begin chronicling the fruits of her newly acquired faith—she shifts narrative focus from herself to her husband, who embodies, at least initially, the full range of all eighteenth-century anti-Quaker sentiment. By making her husband the main protagonist at this point, Ashbridge creates a textual situation in which she can maintain the same self-image that she has established from the beginning. Through this strategy, she continues to characterize herself as a seeker who searches for belonging and attachment but continues to be alienated, abused, and alone. This narrative shift links Ashbridge's spiritual journey with its analogous secular and more private journey, and in so doing, it connects the two layers of the text—the conversion narrative and the autobiography.

Like her spiritual journey, Ashbridge's secular journey begins when she leaves her home and her parents, determined to make a life of her own. Yet despite assertions of independence, her need for attachments to replace those she left behind dominates her story. In the voice of the autobiographer, not that of the conversion narrator, Ashbridge recounts a series of extraordinary experiences that reveal her longing for connectedness.

Ashbridge says she decided to emigrate from the British Isles to separate herself from her father geographically as well as emotionally, yet the sections of the narrative detailing the preparation for the voyage and the crossing itself are filled with evidence of her need for human bonding at the very time when she was severing the few ties that remained. In each of the bizarre events that she describes, her attempts at bonding failed, leading to disillusionment and a growing sense of alienation and loneliness.

In her early negotiations for passage on board a ship, for example, Elizabeth met "a Gentlewoman that then lately came from Pennsylvania (& was going back again)," and she negotiated an indenture contract with this woman to pay for her transportation (150). Much to her surprise and dismay, this woman was not so gentle as she seemed. Luring Elizabeth to a ship under the pretense of showing her their travel accommodations, the woman turned on her and held her captive on board the ship for more than three weeks.[10] While confined, Elizabeth shared her quarters with another captive, "a Young Woman I afterward understood was of a very good Family, and had been deluded away by this creature," whom Ashbridge believes would have been such "an agreeable Companion" (150). Finding companionship seemed to concern her as much as did the predicament of her captivity. Looking back on this episode she chose words that make her captor and cocaptive not kidnapper and victim but two more actors in a long line of potential relationships gone awry.

Even the voyage itself, which Elizabeth was finally able to arrange after several weeks delay, contributed to her growing sense of being alone. She remembers her crossing as yet another example of her inability to form attachments and to find a sense of community. Crowded onto the ship were "Sixty Irish Servants . . . & several English Passengers," along with the Pennsylvanian kidnapper, "the Gentlewoman beforementioned & a Young Man her Husband's Brother" (150–51). Having become fluent in the Irish language while in Ireland, Elizabeth overheard a mutiny plot being hatched by the Irish servants and "discovered their barbarous design privately to the Captain" (151). Unfortunately, the captain was not so grateful for her efforts at saving the lives of himself and his crew as she had hoped. He rewarded her by forcing her to sign an illegal indentureship agreement before disembarking in New York.[11] Recounting this episode, Ashbridge seems almost more upset that the bond she anticipated between the captain and herself did not materialize than she is by the actual events. Ashbridges' inclusion of this incident in her narrative thus emphasizes her feelings of betrayal and alienation: "those to whom I had been Instrumental under Providence to save Life, proved Treacherous to me: I was a Stranger in a Strange Land" (151).

Descriptions of crossing the Atlantic in both directions are common in Quaker ministers' narratives, yet once again Ashbridge's text bears little resemblance to those of her contemporaries. For example, when Catherine Phillips describes her voyage to America, she catalogs rough weather, seasickness, and a wet bed from a leaky ship (63–64), not kidnapping, physical abuse, and illegal indenture. Where Phillips's voyage centers on a priest's regular prayer meetings (67), Ashbridge's crossing is dominated by a murderous mutiny plot. For Phillips, the voyage is an inconvenience; for Ashbridge, it is a disaster. Literally as well as symbolically, Ashbridge's voyage is a break from homeland, family, and any economic security she might have had and the first step toward a life as "a Stranger in a Strange Land."

Ashbridge's recounting of her first years in the American colonies reinforces the tension between her need to be close to someone and her alienation. Less than two weeks after the ship arrived in New York, the shipmaster sold her contract to a cruel, hypocritical man, who "would seem to be a Very Religious Man, taking the Sacrament (so called), & used to Pray every Night in his family" but treated her in a vicious way "that would make the most stony heart pity the Misfortunes of a young creature as [she] was." Ashbridge records abuses ranging from suffering the indignity of wearing clothes that were not "decent," to walking barefoot in the winter, to nearly being whipped by her master (151–52).

Accounts of indentureship in other spiritual autobiographies from this period show that many of Ashbridge's contemporaries also had less than ideal circumstances during servitude. When Jane Hoskens writes of signing her indentureship papers, for example, she recalls her apprehension at being bound to "an utter stranger" with a "mercenary will" who was inclined to abuse the terms of their contract and make "considerable advantage to himself." Although Hoskens describes herself as being "a poor young creature among strangers, and being far separated from [her] natural friends they could not redress [her] grievances nor hear [her] complaints" (6), she remembers this period as a time of hope. Despite her desperate circumstances, she met new friends who offered to help her earn money to pay off her contract and eventually aided her in finding four kind families willing to purchase the remaining years of her service. These families became a source of security; they were "sober and religious men and women" with children who "afforded comfort" to her, families with whom she "served [her] time faithfully, and never had cause to repent it" (7). For Hoskens, the risks and cruelties of indentureship loomed large as threats to her happiness, but that happiness was ultimately retained through the aid of her community of friends. For Ashbridge, the cruelties became reality, and her indentureship was made even more miserable by the lack of friends.

Ashbridge writes of only one friendship during her servitude, formed with a woman who became her confidante. She told this individual of a "difference" with her master that had happened two years earlier, a "difference" that Ashbridge never names but most probably centered on her resistance to her master's sexual advances.[12] Upon hearing that Elizabeth had spoken of these advances, the master

> sent for the Town Whipper to Correct me. I was Called In; he never asked me Whether I had told any such thing but ordered me to strip; at which my heart was ready to burst; for I could as freely have given up my Life as Suffer such Ignominy. I then said if there be a God, be graciously Pleased to Look down on one of the most unhappy Creatures & plead my Cause for thou knows what I have said is the truth; and were it not for a principle more noble than he was Capable of I would have told it before his wife. (153–54)

Although she narrowly escaped the whipping by invoking the name of her father, whose reputation seemed to have influence over her captor, she knew that someone she trusted had betrayed her. Once again Elizabeth felt alone and alienated.

During this same period, Elizabeth tried joining another community by flirting briefly with a career in the theater. A group of New York actors "took a Great fancy" to her and, attempting to persuade her "to become an Actress amongst them," offered to find "means to get [her] from [her] cruel Servitude" so that she might "Live Like a Lady" (153). Finding their proposal attractive, she studied plays late into the night and "used no small Pains to Qualify [her] Self for it." Although "Counted a fine Singer & Dancer" by her new friends, she still rejected this career and served three years of her indentureship until she earned enough money through needlework to purchase the last year of her contract (153). She refused a life on the stage because of her concern with what her father would think when he heard of it. While her desire for friendship and community was strong, the relationship she most wanted was the one she had abandoned at age fourteen.

When Elizabeth married Sullivan, she heightened her search for belonging as her journey became a forced march through New England and the middle colonies. Ashbridge's listing of the places they lived and visited reads like an attempt to find some pattern in or to exert some narrative control over a journey whose seemingly random path she could not alter. The more Sullivan transported his wife across the colonies, the more she craved rootedness and intensified her spiritual search. Elizabeth's mobility may have furthered her spiritual journey by offering the opportunity to experiment with, and then to reject, several denominational affiliations. This process ultimately brought her nearer to accepting Quakerism. But if it facilitated her spiritual quest, the trek across colonial America effectively destroyed her search for friendship and a surrogate family. Sullivan prevented his wife from remaining in one place long enough to form relationships and, therefore, forced her to rely only on him for emotional support. Her second marriage thus became one more roadblock on her path to belonging.

Ashbridge's spiritual journey was also fraught with impediments, but its outcome was more positive because obstacles were overcome. The Devil—"the old accuser," "the crooked serpent"—tempted her at the road's every turn, but God remained a ready ally in her fight. In her account, the spiritual quest becomes a battle for her soul between Satan and God. When "the unwearied adversary" deluded her by making a "false" religion seem attractive, God intervened and moved her toward the Quaker truth. When "the Enemy" tempted her to "End [her] Miserable Life," his power was strong enough to bring her to the garret where she intended to hang herself. Yet, almost immediately upon entering the place, "Horrour seized to that degree, [she] trembled much," and she heard a voice and felt the power of God (153). In the tradition of Quaker autobiography, Ashbridge also recalls a dream of a "heavenly Vision" of a lady with a lamp who kept her from being "caught in another Snare, which if [she] had would Probably have been [her] ruin" (153). Even seemingly minor sins became evidence of the cosmic battle between God and the Devil. While a guest in a Rhode Island home, for example, Elizabeth, alone in a room full of flax, was tempted to steal some so that she might spin some thread:

> I went to it & took a small Bunch in my hand, at which I was smote with remorse. Being of such a kind that my Very Nature abhored it, laid it Down, saying, "Lord keep me from such a Vile Action as this"; but the twisting serpent did not Leave me yet, but Assaulted again so strong & prevalent that I took it into my own Room; but when I came there Horror Seized me, & bursting into Tears Cryed, "Oh thou God of Mercy, enable me to resist this Temptation," which he in his Mercy did. (155)

Whether the temptations are major ones, like suicide, or minor, like stealing flax, God wins the battle for Elizabeth Ashbridge's soul, and her spiritual journey ends happily.

Unfortunately, the same happy ending is not apparent in her search for social belonging. At the end of the narrative, Elizabeth is a woman widowed for the second time, and this time her widowhood is made more tragic because of an ironic twist: she realizes only after Sullivan's death that by living her life as a daily testimony to Quaker teachings she had in fact brought her antagonistic husband to see a glimmering of the Quaker truth. While a soldier in Cuba, Sullivan took his first and last stand for his new beliefs:

> When they Came to prepare for an Engagement, he refused to fight; for which he was whipt and brought before the General, who asked him why he Enlisted if he would not fight; "I did it," said he, "in a drunken frolick, when the Divel had the Better of me, but my judgement is convinced that I ought not, neither will I whatever I Suffer; I have but one Life, & you may take that if you Please, but I'll never take up Arms."—They used him with much Cruelty to make him yield but Could not, by means whereof he was So Disabled that the General sent him to the Hospital at Chelsea, where in Nine Months time he Died & I hope made a Good End. (170)

Only after his death did Elizabeth realize that the kind of marriage relationship she longed for might indeed have been possible with her second husband. Yet, once again, she was alone, separated from the possibility of fulfillment.

Spiritually, Ashbridge thrived; in her daily life, she only survived. The incidents the autobiographer chooses for her self-characterization show her strength, perseverance, and ability to survive endless abuses, yet they also reveal her sense of being an isolated woman. Despite her constant search for attachment and a sense of belonging to replace those that she lost on leaving home, she remains alienated and alone throughout the narrative. While Ashbridge the Quaker writer speaks from a position of centeredness, as autobiographer she can speak only from the margins.

✳

As a young girl, Elizabeth Sampson saw little of her father. From her birth until she was twelve years old, her father was at sea serving as a ship's surgeon. Two years after his return, she left home with an impoverished stocking weaver. Yet years later, as Elizabeth Ashbridge writes her autobiography, she remembers her father's dominant influence over her life. For example, when the man to whom she is indentured threatened to have her whipped, her father's name sprang immediately to her lips and saved her from a beating. When offered a career on the New York stage, she rejected it, choosing instead to remain an indentured servant, because she feared her father's disapproval. When she faced major crises and decisions, the figure of her father surfaced repeatedly. Although she emigrated from her homeland to put distance between them, she could not ignore his power in her life. When her father apparently "had forgiven [her] Disobedience in marrying and earnestly desiring to see [her] again had sent for [her] home," Elizabeth's pride "would not Consent to return in so mean a Condition" (153). So strong was the need for her father's blessing that she chose bondage and alienation over the chance to return home in a state of disgrace.

Read with Elizabeth's almost obsessive concern for paternal approval in the foreground, the narrative becomes a complicated critique of the patriarchal culture in which she lived. If her father's sanction is the voice of that system, she rebels against it, longs for it, and cooperates with it. Her father and the patriarchal system he represents both embody the belonging and connectedness she needs and preclude her from attaining independence and a sense of self-worth.

Living as she did in a patriarchy, Ashbridge's obsession with her father can be partially understood in its cultural context. Eighteenth-century women had no legal or social status apart from the men in their lives. Except as widows, they were allowed no ownership of property (Salmon, *Women* 15), and their only social standing came from taking on "the class of their father or husband, a precarious classless position easily revoked by separation, dispossession, or death" (Nussbaum, *Heteroclites* 149). However, trading the status she had as a surgeon's daughter for that of a poor stocking weaver's wife was not the act of a woman motivated by social standing. Her concern for Dr. Sampson's approval rings truer as an expression of an only daughter's love and admiration for a father she seldom saw.

Ashbridge describes a series of relationships with male authority figures who appear as potential substitutes for the father she misses. When she left home, she traded the love of her father for the love of her young husband. When this husband died, she looked to ministers and to strangers such as the sea captain, with whom she could potentially form bonds. The sea captain in turn sold her to cruel master, who thus forced her to accept his authority. When her indenture was paid off, she immediately married Sullivan, even though she felt no love for him.

The language in which Ashbridge describes these substitutions for her father places her in a submissive role. We can presume that Elizabeth Sampson was attracted to the young stocking weaver, whom she calls "the Darling of [her] Soul," yet she describes eloping as being "carried off in the night" to be married before her parents could "recover" her (148). This is the vocabulary of abduction rather than romance, the young man more a captor than a lover. The rhetoric of victimization thus undercuts the role of willing bride that her actions imply. The marriage that promised attachment and belonging becomes, from the narrator's retrospective view, an act remembered primarily because it separated and alienated Elizabeth from her family.

In the narrative, Ashbridge's second marriage also strengthens the themes of alienation, separation, and bondage. She describes this marriage, coming as it does at the end of her indenture, as one more period of servitude: "I was not Sufficiently Punished; I had got released from one cruel Servitude & then not Contented got into another, and this for Life" (153–54). This comparison between servitude and her marriage to Sullivan is not merely an offhand comment, for the account of that marriage bears many similarities to the description of her period of bondage. She characterizes both the marriage and the indentureship as captivity rather than as the voluntary association that the marriage clearly was. She describes their frequent travels throughout the colonies not as positive moves toward something, but, like her emigration from England, as separations from community or from potential communities. In cataloging their progression through the colonies, Ashbridge writes of "being removed," again casting herself in the role of a passive victim, not unlike the victims of Indian captivity who write of their numerous "removes" from one camp to the next. Rhetorically she becomes her husband's baggage more than his companion.

In recounting Sullivan's treatment of her, Ashbridge emphasizes an image of herself that resonates throughout her text: as property or as a commodity to be bought and sold. Her experiences on the ship and as an indentured servant make this self-image understandable. Ashbridge portrays herself only partly as victim, however, and stresses her own agency in many of the incidents that bring her to this state. She recognizes that she has been an actor and not simply the passive victim; she has made life choices that have been at least partly responsible for her current state.[13] Even in the depths of despair, she continues to accept responsibility for her own unhappiness:

> When I went alone, I used to throw off my apron & garters, & if I had a knife cast it from me Crying, "Lord keep me from taking that Life thou gave, & which thou Would have made happy if I had on my Part joyned with the Offers of Thy Grace, and had regarded the Convictions attending me from my youth: the fault is my own, thou O Lord art clear." (157)

Moreover, as Ashbridge's autobiographical voice continually suggests, Elizabeth played an unusual role in her own abduction, captivity, and commodification.

Examples of Elizabeth's complicity are plentiful. If her elopement appeared to the autobiographer an abduction, the teenaged Elizabeth Sampson, from all indications, was a willing participant in that kidnapping. Although forced into signing illegal indentureship papers on board the ship, she had previously signed them freely for the woman kidnapper. Similarly, once bound to her New York master, she participated in the commodification of herself by purchasing the last year of her own contract, thereby literally buying herself.

How could a woman like Elizabeth, who demonstrated repeated strength and resilience under extraordinary abuses, willingly participate in her own victimization? To be sure, the patriarchy in which she lived severely limited her options. But her intense desire for belonging and human attachment also provide a key to her seemingly inexplicable behavior. With her efforts at genuine human bonding thwarted at every turn—albeit often by her own actions and choices—becoming a captive or property provided another variety of attachment. Ownership becomes the only kind of belonging Elizabeth knew, and she had evidence of its greater stability. The stocking weaver died after only five months of marriage, but her indentureship lasted its full term. Preferring attachment without love to no attachment at all, she married Sullivan, hoping at least to find this same kind of security and stability. For Ashbridge, losing the attachment to her father created an abyss in her life; she chose not to be without some connectedness again.

When Ashbridge experienced conversion, she found in God the ultimate father figure and the security that allowed her to firmly assert her priorities to Sullivan:

> I then Drew up my resolution & told him as a Dutyfull Wife ought, So I was ready to obey all his Lawfull Commands, but where they Imposed upon my Conscience, I no longer Durst: For I had already done it too Long, & wronged my Self by it, & tho' he was near & I loved him as a Wife ought, yet *God was nearer than all the World to me,* & had made me sensible this was the way I ought to go, the which I Assured him was no Small Cross to my own will, yet *had Given up My heart,* & hoped that he that Called for it would Enable me the residue of my Life to keep it steadyly devoted to him, whatever I Suffered for it, adding I hoped not to make him any the worse Wife for it. (165–166, emphasis added)

Again Ashbridge substitutes in the narrative one authority figure for another. Although she pledges dutiful submission to Sullivan, that duty is not her primary one. The language she chooses shows that God—not Sullivan—is her real love.[14]

Sullivan recognizes her new allegiance and responds with the jealousy of a lover scorned. He heaps abuses upon her, ranging from more passive measures, such as depriving her of a horse and therefore making her walk long distances to meeting, to active threats of violence: "he once came up to me & took out his pen knife saying, 'if you offer to go to Meeting tomorrow, with this knife I'll cripple you, for you shall not be a Quaker'" (166). These are the actions of a man who knows that he is not the object of his wife's devotion.

With this final substitution of God for Sullivan, Ashbridge has come full circle. If reconciliation with Dr. Sampson is still impossible, she has at least found a spiritual father to give her a sense of security and belonging. More to the point of her narrative, she finds this father figure within a tradition that deemphasizes patriarchy and empowers women by encouraging them to speak. While she must continue to live her daily life within the dominant patriarchal culture, her Quakerism implicitly critiques that system and offers her the security of a father without requiring passivity.

In childhood Elizabeth wished she had been a boy so that she could be a minister and therefore be "beloved of God" (148). With her new position in the Quaker meeting, her wish is partially realized. Not only does she love God, but she feels that love returned. This father welcomes her instead of turning her away. Having moved from father to stocking weaver to sea captain to master to Sullivan to God, and finding the ultimate sense of belonging and attachment only in God, it is little wonder that she stops writing before her third marriage to Aaron Ashbridge. How could she remain the exemplary Quaker and replace God?

✳

Elizabeth Ashbridge unifies her autobiography by creating continuity where little existed. Her narrative strategies connect her early years of rebellion against parental authority and her years as a new Quaker married to an abusive husband by suggesting that all these experiences contributed to making her the successful Quaker preacher of her later years. Yet even as she emphasizes continuity, her autobiography is also a conversion narrative and is thus, by definition, a story of change. The thematic and narrative consistency that Ashbridge achieves is grounded largely in a series of life changes. Physical and geographical changes throughout her life prevent her from bonding with the communities she seeks. Change becomes her only constant, and paradigmatic change, in the form of religious conversion, becomes her central reason for writing the narrative. Ashbridge's search for narrative continuity mirrors the quest for personal unity that she finally found in Quakerism. Her conversion to that faith provided one kind of unity; the Quakers' insistence on living life in the world instead of apart from it gave her the imperative to try to discover the same kind of unity throughout her life. She found it through the act of writing her spiritual autobiography. While the genre gave her the formula for articulating her newly found religious unity, however, it could not show her how to make sense of the unusual experiences of her life and how to bring her early life into harmony with her later success as a Quaker minister. Ashbridge faced the creative challenge of finding some sort of connectedness between her public and private life, finding consistency throughout the myriad changes she had experienced.

That she chose not to account for some of the most major life changes does not imply a failure in the face of this creative challenge. To be sure, closure is absent from her narrative, and her story is incomplete. Although Aaron Ashbridge proclaims his wife's prominence and tells of her later adventures in her "service of the Truth," Elizabeth tells us nothing of her own successes, discontinuing her story at the point when she learns of Sullivan's death. Because of the dictates of her faith, however, closure *must* be absent, for conversion to the Quaker faith is an ongoing process rather than a finite experience. Following convincement, a Quaker is expected to lead a life growing daily in sanctification and closeness to the truth. Ashbridge's narrative could not express closure, because as a good Quaker she cannot have experienced it, but she could demonstrate a life led according to her newfound faith.

By making Sullivan the predominant character in the last part of the text, Ashbridge represents herself as a good Quaker. As Daniel Shea has insightfully argued, her narrative strategies not only document the moral action of the narrator, but they are part of her moral actions. By choosing to remain silent about Sullivan's abhorrent treatment, letting his actions speak for themselves while commenting only on her growing love for him, the narrator demonstrates the power of love and benevolence that the Quakers preach (Shea 36–39). The narrative act itself becomes part of her process of living a sanctified life. Her narrative choices, whether conscious or instinctive, are sophisticated in that they allow her both to demonstrate her growing sanctification and to create a sense of unity in her character.

In the consistency of change, Elizabeth Ashbridge finds her identity. At times in her text that identity is one of a strong woman able to endure upheavals and to thrive in the wake of overwhelming changes. At other times her identity almost seems evidence of a dysfunctional personality, for as she constantly reminds us, many of her trials resulted from her own choices. Ashbridge lived her life on the margins, and, at least some of the time, she placed herself on these edges. Ashbridge's focus on this marginalization is yet another sophisticated narrative choice that subtly reinforces her reputation as an exemplary Quaker—perhaps even more exemplary than some of her contemporaries who use their narratives to place themselves firmly within the Quaker mainstream.

By the early eighteenth century, Quakers, though still a growing population, had to come to terms with the realization that they would never be the majority and that however powerful an influence they exerted in Pennsylvania, they would never be the dominant culture William Penn had envisioned.[15] By the time Ashbridge became a Quaker, the Society of Friends not only recognized itself as a minority, but Quakers had already begun to enforce their sense of otherness by setting themselves apart through dress, language, and behavior. Ashbridge wrote her spiritual autobiography for a community that had internalized this sense of being a group set apart, and, as she tells us in her text, Quaker practices governed her own life. Facing the problem of how to characterize herself, she had this communal norm as her model. In this context, the image of Elizabeth Sampson Sullivan Ashbridge as a woman on the margins of society is a distinctively Quaker mode of characterization. Thus, even in the private autobiographical act of self-creation, Ashbridge's narrative fulfills its public function as a Quaker text.

5

Gender, Genre, and Cultural Positions

Elizabeth

Ashbridge

and John

Woolman

No historical study of eighteenth-century British North America can reasonably ignore the Quaker presence in the middle colonies. As the Ashbridge family's success illustrates, Quakers in Pennsylvania, New Jersey, and New York at the time assumed leadership positions in government, finance, commerce, and education, as well as within the organizational structure of the Quaker meeting. In journals, diaries, conversion narratives, and letters they left written records of their achievements, as well as of their piety. Until recently, however, only one of these documents—John Woolman's *Journal*—has received the attention of literary critics and historians.

Now frequently anthologized, Woolman's *Journal* provides ample evidence that eighteenth-century colonial society was more complex than the common, but too simple, division between the sacred world of Jonathan Edwards and the secular world of Benjamin Franklin would allow. That schematic has explicitly or implicitly guided criticism, literary history, and anthology production since the beginning of the twentieth century.[1] As Woolman's text reveals, Quaker experience brought the sacred and the secular into a necessary and inescapable conjunction. It suggests the inadequacy inherent in the dualistic opposition of church versus state, while complicating and enriching our understanding of the period's literature and culture.

Elizabeth Ashbridge's narrative further complicates our understanding. If Woolman's journal has become a touchstone of sorts for any study of eighteenth-century Quaker narrative—indeed, for the study of American narrative in general—reading Ashbridge's autobiographical text with Woolman's serves as a pointed reminder of the diversity of Quaker experience.

That Ashbridge and Woolman shared the same cultural and social context enriches a comparison of their personal narratives. Ashbridge (1713–1755) and Woolman (1720–1772) were contemporaries whose influence as Quaker preachers spanned the same historical period and geographical area in colonial North America. Although no extant evidence links them in conversation or correspondence, details from their narratives make it probable that they would have known of each other, and perhaps even have met, in New Jersey. Ashbridge writes that during the later years of her marriage to Mr. Sullivan, they moved to Mount Holly, New Jersey, where they both taught school (169). Although the date of their move is undocumented, Ashbridge recounts that they lived in Mount Holly long enough to work at their respective teaching jobs and to acquire and to furnish a house before 1740, when Sullivan enlisted in the army and left home (169). Although she mentions nothing about her whereabouts after Sullivan's departure, Aaron Ashbridge, in his note appended to her narrative, indicates that Sullivan "had been gone some two or three Years before she had a Certain Account of his Death," and that upon his death, he left Elizabeth in debt (171). The combination of Elizabeth's lack of information about her husband, her lack of money, and her lack of connectedness to her parents makes it plausible that she remained in Mount Holly in her "Prettily furnished" home (169) and continued teaching. During this same period, John Woolman, then twenty-one years old, left his parents' home for the first time to "tend shop and keep books" for a man in Mount Holly (29).[2] Although his early life in Mount Holly predates his renown within the Quaker community, he writes of attending meeting in his new home and even of speaking for the first time in the meeting (31). These details suggest his familiarity with the Quaker community, which at the time probably still included Elizabeth Sullivan.

If an Ashbridge-Woolman connection remains tantalizing but tenuous during her lifetime, more tangible evidence documents Woolman's knowledge of Ashbridge after her death in Ireland in 1755. Woolman writes that during a 1758 visit to several Pennsylvania meetings, he, along with two other visiting Friends, "had a family meeting at our friend's Aaron Ashbridge's" (94). While we can only speculate about what was discussed during this visit, a letter from Aaron Ashbridge to Israel Pemberton, another prominent Quaker, indicates that Elizabeth's narrative may have been part of the conversation.[3] This 1757 letter, written prior to Woolman's visit, accompanied a copy of Elizabeth's narrative. Aaron told Pemberton that he enclosed for his perusal "some memorials which my late Dear Wife left in her own handwriting." He asked that Pemberton circulate them among other members of the Quaker community, particularly to "John Woolman at Mount Holly, who hath requested the perusal thereof." As Daniel Shea has observed, this letter documents the interconnections of the literary culture within which Quaker autobiographers wrote, and it thus provides the opportunity to think about Woolman's *Journal* not only as the work that influenced other Quaker writers, but also as a work that may itself have been influenced by writers such as Elizabeth Ashbridge (*Journeys* 138).

Amid the generic similarities of Woolman's journal and Ashbridge's narrative, however, striking differences appear. These differences show the diversity of individual Quaker experience despite the strong group identity characteristic of the Society of Friends. While Ashbridge and Woolman shared the culture of Quakerism, their narratives demonstrate their reliance on vocabularies from more than one cultural tradition to convey their experience. Although the Quaker meeting emphasized the equality of men and women, Woolman's and Ashbridge's vocabularies are most certainly gendered, and despite the meeting's belief in the equality of men and women, gender colors their experiences as Quakers. Yet attributing all the disparities between these narratives to gender would ignore other equally powerful circumstances in the authors' lives that position them in different relationships to Quakerism. For Woolman, being born to a supportive Quaker family, spending his entire adolescence with that family, and growing up within the fold of the meeting allowed him to take for granted a sense of belonging that Ashbridge spent her life searching for. Differences inherent in Ashbridge's self-identification as an outsider and in Woolman's experiences as an insider merge with eighteenth-century cultural constructions of gender to distinguish these two personal narratives and their narrators.

✳

Initially, the similarities between these narratives may seem to over-shadow their differences. Both Ashbridge and Woolman understood their Quakerism and, indeed, defined their relationship to their faith in terms of separation and difference from the dominant non-Quaker culture, a tenet central to the institutional history of Quakerism. By emphasizing their "otherness," Quakers like Ashbridge and Woolman became part of the tradition of sectarian dissent that R. Laurence Moore places at the heart of the American religious experience. In *Religious Outsiders and the Making of Americans,* Moore uses the Mormons as his case study. Although theirs is essentially a nineteenth-century story, the Mormon experience shares much with that of eighteenth-century Quakers, and Moore's analysis provides useful insights into Quaker cultural history.

The Mormons, Moore argues, self-consciously constructed a sense of otherness in order to define themselves as a distinct people. "They had to invent an identity for themselves and that required them to maintain certain fictions of cultural apartness" (32). Although they shared with the dominant middle class the values of thrift, frugality, and hard work, the Mormons nonetheless emphasized practices set-ting them apart from the mainstream. According to Moore:

> Mormons were different because they said they were different and because their claims, frequently advanced in the most obnoxious way possible, prompted others to agree to treat them as such. (31)

Eventually the Mormons' efforts at self-definition led to persecution. Early Mormon newspapers featured accounts of religious persecution, which Moore contends became "the distinctive badge of membership in the church; it was the test of faith and one's chosenness" (34). This oppositional stance, Moore argues, "gives value to struggle and incul-cates self-confidence" while creating a sense of peoplehood within the Mormon community (35).

Like the Mormons, eighteenth-century Quakers were concerned with self-consciously creating themselves as a people through opposi-tion to the dominant culture with which they nevertheless shared many values. Unlike the Mormons, whose community was more geographically bounded, the Quakers needed a communal definition strong enough to span the Atlantic, and their separateness had to be visible to the varied cultures of England, Ireland, and colonial North America. Public Friends traveling back and forth across the Atlantic could easily reinforce uniformity among Quakers, but their markers of distinction were chosen carefully to be both consistent with Quaker testimony and different from all of the dominant cultures surrounding them.

Maintaining distinctiveness was a particular problem for eighteenth-century Quakers in the North American colonies, where they faced temptations to blend in with other Protestant dissenters, many of whom shared the Quaker preference for simplicity. One means by which the Quaker meetings dealt with this problem was by establishing schools designed to seclude the children of Friends, thereby protecting them from the contaminating influence of the heathen world. Believing that the future of Quakerism depended on the young, Friends struggled to maintain these schools despite a consistent shortage of schoolmasters after 1700 (Frost 74ff).[4]

Separate schools for Quakers and the ideology surrounding them make it clear that the history of Quakerism is largely corporate rather than individualistic. While the Inner Light empowered individuals, it also inevitably led to a communal ethos and a shared life among those who had experienced it. Just as Ashbridge struggled to create an authentic self-definition in her autobiography, the Quakers as a whole searched for an identity to define and to unify themselves as a people. Quaker theology may emphasize the individual, but the daily lives of Friends stressed the communal identity of a people set apart.

Although creating an identity in opposition to the larger society undoubtedly united the Quaker community, it also led to a central tension within Friends' daily lives. Acting like a people set apart by withdrawing from the world was not an option for Quakers. Their teachings stressed the importance of being *of* the world, participating in it as fully as their beliefs would allow, and thereby spreading the benefits of the Inner Light to the larger society. Being true to their tenets required that Quakers be a people at once segregated from the world and still within that world, for only by making a contribution to society could they become good Quakers.

This tension in Quakerism between reforming the world and

escaping from it to form a holy community surfaces often in Quaker writing. The faith's precepts of order, industry, and frugality served Friends well in eighteenth-century America, making them successful merchants, professionals, and government officials.[5] However, their achievements, particularly in Pennsylvania and New Jersey, threatened to submerge them in the dominant culture against which they defined themselves. Their prominence thus endangered their spiritual identity as a people set apart; however, retreating from their civic responsibilities would have made impossible their hopes of reforming the world through example. For the devout Quaker, the desire to do good constantly conflicted with the experience of doing well.[6]

This central drama in the corporate history of Quakerism played itself out differently in the lives of both Woolman and Ashbridge. Each brought to the debate differing relationships to the world outside of the meeting and distinct notions of what it meant to participate in that world. For Woolman, being of the world meant, in large part, being successful within the community in which he was raised. As his move to Mount Holly to tend shop for a merchant and his later decision to become a tailor demonstrate, Woolman had both the requisite financial resources and the community sanction to enter the mercantile world and to pursue a successful career. Quakers and non-Quakers alike supported his efforts at beginning a career in their community. Ashbridge, however, lacked any such opportunity for financial advancement. Being of the world for her meant being of Sullivan's world, a realm of abuse, captivity, and alienation. As a woman she had limited options for marking her success in the world outside the Quaker meeting. Her sense of the myriad debates about the nature of Quakerism, which she heard and undoubtedly participated in during meetings, was necessarily filtered through these life experiences.

The realities of gender and of her self-definition as an outsider color Ashbridge's understanding of the very nature of Quakerism and of the communal definition of a "peculiar people" set apart from the world in which they must also succeed. Woolman, raised with a sense of belonging to the Quaker community and enjoying social and cultural privilege that Ashbridge lacked, could approach questions of otherness philosophically and with some sense of choice about how and to what extent he would implement and manipulate the markers of

Quaker distinctiveness. Ashbridge lacked the luxury of such options. To Ashbridge, far from a philosophical debate, these markers and her skill in manipulating them were essential to survival.

✳

In Quaker culture, as well as in the narratives of Ashbridge and Woolman, the drama of worldly success versus exemplary piety was staged most visibly in the material environment, the things that surrounded Friends in their daily lives. Clothing, furniture, architecture, language, and behavior formed the boundaries between "strict" Quakers—those who adhered rigorously to standards of simplicity—and "wet" Quakers—those who lived more lavish lives.[7] These indicators of Quakerism in everyday life provide an important key to understanding what it meant to be a peculiar people. They also facilitate analysis of the different manifestations of Quakerism in the lives of Ashbridge and Woolman.

The importance that Quakers placed upon their material surroundings follows logically from their testimony of simplicity—a testimony that led them to shun anything unnecessary, particularly embellished speech, exaggerated behavior, or any superfluous ornamentation on clothing, furniture, or architecture. More than an affectation, their concern for the plain style was inextricably tied to their testimony of equality and to a concern for social justice. Conspicuous consumption by those who could afford fancy decoration not only emphasized economic stratification, a reality the Quakers tried to avoid, but, as William Penn argued, it also deprived the poor: "The very trimming of the vain world would clothe all the naked one" (Tolles, *Quakers* 77). Seemingly designed to downplay the materiality of Friends' lives, their emphasis on simplicity and equality, paradoxically, had the opposite effect. How could the meeting judge which members were and which were not living a plain life except by looking at these very markers? Quakers' success or failure at eliminating material concerns from their lives could be judged only by directing individual and communal attention to the materiality of everyday life that they wished to avoid.[8]

The importance of material culture to the corporate enterprise of Quakerism is evident both in Ashbridge's narrative and in Woolman's journal. Each narrator keenly understands how the material environment, especially clothing, functions as a system of symbols for Quakers and non-Quakers alike. These signs, for example, could signal an ever-deepening commitment to the Inner Light. Quakers' awareness of the symbolic power of material goods follows logically from the plethora of advice and admonitions Quaker meetings issued throughout the colonies about how Friends should best live simple lives. Hannah Hill's 1726 letter from women at the Burlington, New Jersey Yearly Meeting to the women of the Chester, Pennsylvania Monthly Meeting typified the suggestions made by Quaker groups. Written with "a weighty concern" for the "divers undue Liberties that are too frequently taken by some" Friends, Hill's letter cautioned against all practices inconsistent with the plain style:

> As first, That Immodest fashion of hooped Pettycoats . . .
> And also That None of Sd friends Accustom themselves to wear their Gowns with Superfluous folds behind, but plain and Decent. Nor to go without Aprons. . . . Nor to wear their heads drest high . . .
> And that friends are careful to avoid Wearing of Stript Shoos, or Red or White heel'd Shoos . . .
> Likewise, That all friends be Careful to Avoid Superfluity of Furniture in thier [*sic*] Houses . . .
> And also that no friends Use the Irreverent practice of taking Snuff, or handing Snuff boxes one to Another in Meetings.
> Also that friends Avoid the Unnecessary use of fans in Meetings. . . .
> And also That friends do not Accustom themselves to go in bare Breasts or bare Necks.
> There is Likewise a Tender Concern upon our minds to recommend unto all friends, the Constant use of the plain Language. . . .

These recommendations must be followed, Hill concluded, if Quakers were to follow the scriptural admonition and become "A Chosen Generation, A Royal Priesthood, An Holy Nation, A Peculair [*sic*] People" (Berkin and Norton 135).

As Hill's letter indicates, plainness in clothing was a major Quaker concern. Friends were admonished not only to eliminate decoration but also to avoid frequent changes of style. Following fashion trends, the Quakers believed, demonstrated vanity and pride. As early as 1667 George Fox preached against high fashion:

> Keep out of the vain fashions of the world; let not your eyes, and minds, and spirits run after every fashion. . . . And Friends that see the world so often alter their fashions, if you follow them, and run into them, in that ye cannot judge the world, but the world will rather judge you. Therefore, keep all in modesty and plainness.
> (Frost 194)

As Fox's admonition suggests, Quaker garments were all too often nearly indistinguishable from those worn by other Protestants, lacking only the ornamentation.

The ever-increasing specificity of advice from the eighteenth-century meetings highlights the continuing struggle faced by Quakers who could too easily accommodate themselves to the non-Quaker culture around them. The regulations from the Philadelphia Meeting in 1704, for example, duplicated and distributed throughout the North American colonies and the British Isles, delineated in amazing detail the specific evils committed by members of the Society of Friends, leaving little room for misinterpreting guidelines for simple dress:

> If any men wear longlapp'd sleeves, or Coats folded at the sides, Superfluous buttons, Broad ribbons about the hat, or gaudy, flower'd or strip'd Stuffs, or any sort of perriwigs unless necessitated, and if any are necessitated, that then it be as near in Colour as may be to their own and in other respects resembling as much as may be, a sufficient natural head of hair without the vain customs being long behind or mounting on the forehead. Also, if any women that profess the Truth wear or suffer their children to wear their Gowns not plain or open at the breast with gaudy Stomachers, needless rolls at the Sleeves or with their Mantuas or Bonnets with gaudy colours, or cut their hair and leave it out on the brow, or dress their heads high, or to wear hoods with long lapps, or long Scarfs open before, or their Capps or pinners plaited or gathered on the brow or double hemm'd or pinch'd. . . . It being not agreeable to that Shamefac'dness, plainness and modesty which people professing Godliness with good works ought to be found in. (Frost 194)[9]

With regulations such as these spewing forth from meetings throughout the colonies, it is little wonder that Quaker ministers, needing to document their exemplary piety, seized on clothing as a readily available shorthand to mark their peculiarity. As their narratives demonstrate, both Woolman and Ashbridge wrote with confidence that their readers would understand the symbolic power of clothing. They use it as a cultural marker to illustrate Quaker distinction. Woolman manipulates his attire in order to heighten the separation between himself and the non-Quaker world around him, thereby providing visual evidence of the strength of his theological and philosophical beliefs. On the other hand, Ashbridge, during the days following her conversion, clings tenaciously to non-Quaker clothing as a desperate means of maintaining some link with the community that Sullivan mandates for her.

Clothing held particular importance for Woolman, a tailor. In addition to monitoring his own dress, he had to be concerned with the boundaries between simplicity and superfluity in the clothing he sewed for others.[10] Plainness in Woolman's own wardrobe ultimately came to mean undyed garments; he believed that "garments dyed with a dye hurtful to them" were superfluous, and superfluities were connected "with some degree of oppression, and with that spirit which leads to self-exultation and strife" (120). Putting his convictions into practice, however, proved difficult. First he worried that his friends would think him "singular" for wearing only natural colors. For a time, therefore, he "remained in the use of some things contrary to [his] judgment" to allay his apprehension (120). When, after much deliberation, he bought "a hat the natural colour of the fur," he learned that similar hats were "in use among some who were fond of following the changeable modes of dress," and he feared that Friends would think he violated the testimony of simplicity by following fashion trends (121). His fears were well-founded, for "some Friends were apprehensive that [his] wearing such a hat savored of an affected singularity" (121).

Potential censure by his fellow Quakers notwithstanding, Woolman carried his concern for simplicity in dress to such extremes that even the Quakers thought him peculiar. Seemingly undaunted by the alienation that such singularity could create for him, Woolman writes of his overriding concern for consistency between his material world and his philosophical convictions. Having already demonstrated his capacity for success in the mercantile world, he had available the

resources and the freedom to pursue the consistency he desired, even
at the expense of decentering himself within the Quaker community.

Already positioned on the margins of society, Ashbridge could
hardly consider any action that would move her further from the center of her world. Recognizing that her dress carried enormous symbolic power and that clothing could instantly mark a woman as different, Ashbridge, like Woolman, manipulated her clothing to make a
statement about her Quakerism. Initially, the statement she needed to
make was one that would quell the fears of the non-Quaker world in
which Sullivan forced her to live rather than one that would proclaim
her piety to Friends. She was necessarily much more concerned about
her safety and the problems of standing out from those around her.
Consequently, she took pains to hide her new beliefs. According to her
narrative, she

> never Let any know the Condition [she] was in, nor did [she]
> appear like a Friend, & fear'd Discovery. . . . But notwithstanding
> all [her] care the Neighbours that were not friends began to revile
> [her], calling [her] Quaker, saying they supposed [she] intended to
> be a fool and turn Preacher. (160)

Still unable to acknowledge the truth of these charges publicly, Elizabeth "in order to Change their Opinions got into greater Excess in
Apparel than [she] had freedom to Wear for some time before [she]
came Acquainted with Friends" (160).[11] She believed that no devout
Quaker would dress to excess and that ornamented attire could, therefore, serve as her disguise. How could a woman dressed this way possi-
bly be suspected of Quakerism? Much to her dismay, the power of the
Inner Light shone through her costume and, as Sullivan dragged her
through the colonies to remove her from the influence of her Quaker
relatives, she was unsuccessful in concealing her new faith. Although
she "still did not appear like a Friend," those to whom her husband
reviled her all recognized her as a troublesome Quaker (161). Later in
their journey, at the home of a "Worthy Friend," Elizabeth was
touched by the kindness shown by her hosts, because she believed
that it could not stem from mere duty or any sense of obligation to
another Quaker: "The friends' kindness could not proceed from my
appearing in the Garb of a Quaker, for I had not yet altered my dress"

(165). Ashbridge realized that clothing could either disguise her Quakerism or announce it to the world.

That Ashbridge used her clothing to conceal her faith while Woolman used his to demonstrate the depth of his faith reflects the differences in the cultural positioning of these two autobiographers. Ashbridge, marginalized and alienated at every point in her early life, signals her perpetual desire for connectedness by attempting, albeit unsuccessfully, to maintain her ties to the people around her. As a man closer to the cultural center, Woolman manipulates the symbolism to reinforce his position of power without apparent concern that he might decenter himself in the process.

Certainly the different cultural locations from which Ashbridge and Woolman write reflect the realities of gender in eighteenth-century American culture, where women were relegated to the cultural margins politically, socially, and economically. Despite Ashbridge's eventual eminence within the Quaker meeting, her life outside of the meeting continued to reinforce her memories of early disconnectedness and subjugation. Even more striking in this comparison is the palpable sense of security interwoven throughout Woolman's *Journal*— a security within his family, within the public world, and within his faith—that allows him the freedom to push at the boundaries of religious practices related to the Quaker testimony of simplicity. Estranged from her family and a new convert to Quakerism, Ashbridge inevitably lacked the same security and the hope of ever attaining it, even to the degree that Woolman could take for granted.

✻

Both Woolman's and Ashbridge's actions in proclaiming Quaker convictions spoke louder than their words. Seventeenth-century Friends had set precedents for them through indefatigable challenges to the Puritan establishment. Martyrs like Mary Dyer are memorable not for what they said, but rather for their relentless demonstrations of the power of the Inner Light. Similarly, Quaker men throughout the eighteenth century continued to suffer humiliation, if not physical abuse, for the testimony of equality by refusing to remove their hats in deference to those in positions of authority. The four Quaker testimonies of simplicity, equality, community, and peace were intended as moral guides for behavior, and Friends knew that when they acted on these principles, they were likely to suffer for their beliefs.

Textually, Woolman and Ashbridge act on the same principles but in different ways. Woolman's narrative strategy depicts events that either trigger a philosophical discussion about the most effective way to integrate his Quaker beliefs and testimonies into his daily life, or show the results of a philosophical decision. These discussions and the religious implications of his actions, rather than the actions themselves, seem most important to him as a narrator trying to demonstrate exemplary piety. Piety and religious commitment can be easily read in the events described in Ashbridge's narrative as well. For Ashbridge, however, the events themselves are important, and she typically recounts them without any accompanying discussions of their significance for her faith.

Early in the autobiographies, the pattern of Woolman's philosophic musings and Ashbridge's personally wrenching experiences emerges. After only a few short paragraphs, Woolman relates the only event between the ninth and twelfth years of his life that he deemed significant enough to include in his journal. Noticing a mother robin and her young in a nest, Woolman "stood and threw stones at her, till one striking her, she fell down dead." After a few moments of reveling in his accomplishment, he was soon "seized with horror, as having in a sportive way killed an innocent creature while she was careful for her young." Feeling some responsibility for the baby birds, he climbed to the nest, removed the birds, and killed them, "supposing that better than to leave them to pine away and die miserably" (24). As one of few childhood memories recorded, this anecdote—a parable for the rest of his text—has importance and usefulness to a narrator seeking to demonstrate the workings of the Inner Light in him even at this young age. Saying only that his actions continued to trouble him several hours later, the narrator finds this event useful as evidence "that Scripture proverb was fulfilled, 'The tender mercies of the wicked are cruel' [Prov. 12:10]" (24–25).

In contrast to Woolman's use of childhood memories as object lessons, Ashbridge relates childhood events that more tangibly and immediately changed her life. For example, while eloping against her parents' wishes could easily become illustrative of scriptural cautions against disobedience, Ashbridge articulates no such parallels. Instead, she presents it as the first in a series of "precipitate action[s]" that "plunged [her] into a deal of Sorrow" (148). If Woolman's memories of the dead robins held powerful meaning for the narrator as a parable, Ashbridge's memory was a strong reminder of the horror of her first experience of separation and alienation.

Woolman's journal provides numerous examples of the personal suffering he faced as a price for acting consonantly with his moral principles. He describes moments when he gave public demonstrations of his private faith, providing useful examples for other Quakers seeking to reconcile their beliefs with their daily lives. Convinced of the evils of slavery, for example, Woolman refused to write legal documents having anything to do with that system. Believing that "it is the duty of everyone to be firm in that which they certainly know is right for them" (50), Woolman had no small amount of difficulty when asked to write a conveyance for slaves (32–33) or a will for a slaveowner (50–51), but he faced an even more complicated moral crisis when a neighbor who was gravely ill asked Woolman to prepare his will.

> I took notes, and amongst other things he told me to which of his children he gave his young Negro. I considered the pain and distress he was in and knew not how it would end, so I wrote his will, save only that part concerning his slave, and carrying it to his bedside read it to him and I then told him in a friendly way that I could not write any instruments by which my fellow creatures were made slaves, without bringing trouble on my own mind. I let him know that I charged nothing for what I had done and desired to be excused from doing the other part in the way he proposed. Then we had a serious conference on the subject, and at length, he agreeing to set her free, I finished his will. (51)

Although Woolman's benevolent feelings toward the man were strong, his belief in promoting Quaker teachings through his actions ultimately governed his decision; and, as he testifies, his faith and powers of friendly persuasion were rewarded by the acquiescence of the slaveowner.

Woolman felt the strength of his convictions tested again when he believed it "required of [him] to be resigned to go on a visit to some parts of the West Indies" (155). The only transport available, however, was "a vessel employed in the West India trade" (157), and he believed that booking passage on board that ship would make him complicitous in the oppression it represented. After days of agonized torment over whether to follow his principles or to listen to the voice within him that required his preaching in Barbados, "it pleased the Lord to visit [him] with a pleurisy" that prevented him from traveling, thus resolving his dilemma (159). Upon his recovery, he again felt called to travel, this time to England. While inspecting the ship on which he was to book passage, however, he noticed "sundry sorts of carved work and imagery" and "some superfluity of workmanship of several sorts" in the cabin. Believing that "the sum of money to be paid for a passage in that apartment hath some relation to the expense of furnishing the room," and that "the moneys received from the passengers are calculated to answer every expense relating to their passage, and amongst the rest, the expense of these superfluities," he "felt a scruple with regard to paying [his] money to defray such expenses." Demonstrating his willingness to suffer personal discomfort in order to preserve his integrity, he chose instead to endure the inconvenience and "unpleasant situation" of a passage in steerage, the only part of the ship free from superfluous ornament (164–65).

While Ashbridge also insisted that her behavior test and demonstrate the depth of her convictions, her actions occur on a more private level than do Woolman's. Like Woolman, she suffered for what she believed. Her refusal to dance in the Wilmington tavern is her most dramatic example of this suffering. As autobiographer, Ashbridge builds up to the tavern scene by using singing and dancing, much as she uses clothing, to mark her movement toward the Inner Light. As a young girl, recently estranged from her father and living with Quaker relatives in Ireland, she finds comfort in being "allowed to sing & dance, which [her] Cousins disallowed of" and characterizes herself as having "great Vivacity in [her] Natural Disposition" and being even "more Wild & Airy than ever" (148–49). While in New York before her conversion, she again notes that she was "Counted a fine Singer & Dancer," talents "in which [she] took great Delight," and which initially attracted Sullivan's attentions (153). Then, in great despair immediately before her conversion, she returns to the musical figures of singing and dancing to dramatize her state of mind:

> My husband was Shock'd, to See me so changed, I that once Could divert him with a Song (in which he greatly delighted), nay after I grew Religious as to the outward, could now Do it no longer. My Singing now was turned into mourning & my Dancing into Lamentations. (156)

The tavern incident thus owes much of its power not only to its inherent dramatic conflict, but also to Ashbridge's command of the event as metaphor, rendering her spiritual state through the sign of her outward behavior.

Discussions of issues like slavery and their far-reaching effects in Quakers' lives, issues so prevalent in Woolman's *Journal,* are absent from Ashbridge's narrative. This lacuna, however, should not surprise her readers. Undoubtedly no less opposed to slavery than Woolman was, Ashbridge would have seen slavery as much more than an occasion for philosophical deliberation and communal censure. Unlike Woolman, Ashbridge knew from her period of indentured servitude what it felt like to be property; she, too, had been bought and sold. Furthermore, as a woman she understood the hopelessness of never being able to become totally independent, always remaining tied financially to a husband. While as a white woman she would never truly understand slavery's horrors, the institution was certainly closer to Ashbridge's experiential realm than it was to Woolman's. For Woolman, slavery became a moral and ethical preoccupation indicative of his ever-increasing commitment to living a life consistent with his Quaker beliefs.

By describing the ways in which slavery touched him personally and the extremes to which he would oppose the institution, Woolman documents the effects of the meeting in his daily life, articulating his understanding of the Quaker principles that changed his life. In so doing, Woolman, self-consciously a public figure, offers his journal as a guide for other members of his faith. Ashbridge, eschewing long philosophical discussions, instead selects events with personal importance to her and presents them with no overt suggestion for the reader. By allowing the strength of her Quaker faith to shine through her actions, she writes a quintessentially Quaker story as well as a powerful autobiography.

✳

Becoming a Quaker created major changes in Ashbridge's world, changes much more radical than those John Woolman describes in his journal. While Woolman gradually harmonized his life with his deepening awareness of what it meant to live according to the Quaker testimonies, he remained a full participant in the larger world; conversely Ashbridge's relationship to the world around her changed suddenly with her conversion. While Woolman altered his dress and behavior in the hope of creating cultural change, Ashbridge manipulated her environment to retard change, allowing herself time to find a balance between the Quaker and non-Quaker worlds that she straddled. In addition to being sudden, the upheaval Ashbridge experienced was even more drastic because she was a woman. From the moment she began to number herself among the Quakers, she had to rethink her understanding of gender and of her role in society.

After Elizabeth entered a Quaker meetinghouse for the first time, her surroundings became gendered in a new way. The spatial configuration of the meetinghouse itself provided a tangible symbol of her changed world. The typical Quaker meetinghouse in the colonies had a simple rectangular floor space with rows of plain benches. During a meeting for worship, the men sat on one side of a central aisle and the women on the other. Ministers and elders sat in front on benches facing the others, with ministers in the top rows and elders beneath them, the men facing the men and the women facing the women. A movable partition divided the room along the central aisle for business meetings, when the men's meeting met independently from the women's.[12] Though the women were separated from the men, their space was equal to the men's space, and positions of prominence at the front of the meetinghouse were filled equally by men and women. In Elizabeth's new world, public places were no longer gendered only as male.

During the meeting for worship, both women and men could address the entire meeting, an act more difficult for women owing to

cultural constraints that habitually silenced women's voices in the public world. At the prospect of speaking in the meeting for the first time,
Ashbridge trembled, knowing that by speaking she would "Confess to
the world what [she] was" (166), and thus take the final step in the
process of disclosure that she had begun after her conversion at the
Pennsylvania home of her Quaker relatives. In Elizabeth's first
encounter with Sullivan after her conversion, her greeting was more
than a welcome. It was a conscious and calculated announcement of
her new status:

> I got up & met him saying, "My Dear, I am glad to see thee," at
> which he flew in a Passion of anger & said, "the Divel thee thee,
> don't thee me." I used all the mild means I could to pacify him, &
> at Length got him fit to go & Speak to my Relations, but he was
> Alarmed. . . ." (161)

Her use of "mild means" to calm Sullivan suggests that Elizabeth—
who had already learned the power of language from her experience
with the Irish mutineers on board the ship—was prepared for his
alarm. Elizabeth's use of the characteristic Quaker speech to greet her
husband amounted to a proclamation of her Quakerism that prefig-
ured the first time she spoke in a Quaker meeting. Both instances were
personally traumatic and centered on speech and language as ways of
publicly asserting convictions. They thus resemble the act of autobiography. From her retrospective view as autobiographer, Ashbridge performed the empowering act of bringing herself to language, and
through language, she found a unified sense of herself.

Woolman's experience of coming to voice differed from Ashbridge's. When he first spoke in the Mount Holly meeting, he experienced no trembling nor hesitancy, but erred instead on the side of
verbosity:

> I stood up and said some words in a meeting, but not keeping close
> to the divine opening, I said more than was required of me; and
> being soon sensible of my error, I was afflicted in mind some weeks
> without any light or comfort. . . . And after this, feeling the spring
> of divine love opened and a concern to speak, I said a few words in
> a meeting, in which I found peace. This I believe was about six

weeks from the first time, and as I was thus humbled and disciplined under the cross, my understanding became more strengthened to distinguish the language of the pure Spirit which inwardly moves upon the heart and taught [me] to wait in silence sometimes many weeks together. (31)

Whereas Ashbridge struggled to overcome the cultural prescriptions against women speaking in public, Woolman battled against his natural inclination for oratory. He had to learn when and how to be silent. Born into the Quaker faith, Woolman never experienced the trauma of disclosing his chosen faith to a hostile audience. As a man who had achieved a level of success in the public world, he never experienced the struggle between culturally imposed silence and the need to bring himself to language. Woolman instead presumed his sanction to speak. His journal amply demonstrates that he perceived his life to be exemplary and believed his deliberations and decisions could be instructional to others. He thus felt it his duty to speak. Elizabeth, however, "thought it [her] duty to say what [she] could in [Sullivan's] Favour," and she thanked God for allowing her to fulfill this duty (170).

Because Woolman and Ashbridge brought to Quaker duty and preaching different perceptions of themselves and their possibilities, the Quaker cultural vocabulary was available to them in different and uneven ways. When they wrote their autobiographical narratives, both were prominent members within a marginalized religious group defined by the metaphor of separation. Woolman, secure with his positions both in the public world and in the meeting and comfortable with the influence they conferred, enjoyed the luxury of experimenting with the real and the metaphorical implications of peculiarity in his daily life. Ashbridge, having lived a life fraught with disconnection, did not understand the Quaker emphasis on separation as metaphor but, rather, as a reality that she had heretofore been powerless to change. To reach a position of prominence as a Quaker preacher, she had to learn to negotiate power and to recognize where she was empowered and where she remained marginalized. Even as she adjusted to the authority accompanying her position within the meeting, she could never escape her continued marginalization within the non-Quaker world.

Consistently aware of how relative her position of prominence had been, Ashbridge's personal narrative testifies to the peculiar power that can be exercised by the marginalized. As Felicity Nussbaum argues:

> [W]omen's autobiographical writing . . . is one location of . . . contradictions that both produce and reflect historicized concepts of self and gender while sometimes threatening to disrupt or transform them. (149)

While Ashbridge continues to rationalize her life through metaphors of separation and dislocation in the narrative, she also demonstrates an ability to negotiate a position of power while still understanding herself as "other." As she exemplifies the effects of eighteenth-century ideologies of gender in her own life, she documents her capacity to "disrupt and transform them" through her success as a Quaker minister. In the act of writing her narrative, Ashbridge illustrates her ability to break the silence imposed on her as an eighteenth-century woman, even as she describes the trauma she has continually faced in bringing herself to language and empowerment. Perhaps owing to this ordeal, Ashbridge could readily persist in challenging societal constraints as she increased her role as a public woman. Through these continued challenges, Ashbridge positioned herself as a foremother for nineteenth-century women who worked toward disrupting the limitations imposed upon them by a world divided into the public sphere of men and the private sphere of women.

6

Elizabeth Ashbridge's Literary Daughters

The Quaker Woman in Nineteenth-Century Fiction

As peculiar people, Elizabeth Ashbridge and her Quaker women contemporaries did much in their daily lives to unsettle eighteenth-century ideologies of gender. By gaining power and prominence through skilled oratory and political leadership within the Quaker meeting and the larger community, women like Ashbridge became increasingly visible proponents of equality. By the nineteenth-century, as boundaries between the Quaker world and the world outside the meetinghouse became less distinct, Friends became less preoccupied with defining themselves through difference, and they found themselves participating in virtually all realms of society. But if nineteenth-century Quaker women no longer seemed so peculiar to those around them, they remained distinctive. In numbers disproportionate to their population, Quaker women distinguished themselves by their leadership in a variety of nineteenth-century reform movements. Authorized by the legacy of women preachers like Ashbridge, they discounted the dominant ideology of separate spheres for men and women and moved into positions of public prominence with an ease denied their non-Quaker contemporaries whose lives were defined by the home. Taking to heart the Friends' egalitarianism, Quaker women enlarged their sphere, believing it their responsibility as well as their right to participate publicly in improving the world around them. Unwilling to accept society's rule that women could influence public events only indirectly through their husbands, fathers, or sons, countless Quaker women in the latter nineteenth century assumed activist positions that allowed them, without male intermediaries, to exert power of their own.

Understanding all types of reform as intrinsically linked in the larger project of effecting positive change in an America working to define and to remake itself as a new nation, Quaker women campaigned in significant numbers for such diverse causes as the abolition of slavery, women's suffrage, Native American rights, prison and housing reform, and the elimination of sweatshop labor.[1] Perhaps most noticeably, they led the earliest efforts to claim women's rights in the new republic, efforts that to many seemed impossible as well as a threat to the very foundations of nineteenth-century social and political life. Four of the five women who planned the 1848 Seneca Falls convention, generally acknowledged as the beginning of the women's movement, were members of the Society of Friends.[2] This planning meeting, staged over tea in a Quaker home, provides dramatic evidence of the way the ideology of separate spheres broke down within the Quaker community, blurring lines between public activism and the private home, and testifying to Quaker prominence—even dominance—in the campaign for women's rights.

With Quaker women playing such visible roles in the unfolding dramas of nineteenth-century social and political movements, and with images and memories of their colonial ancestors still current and powerful in the cultural memory, it should be no surprise that Quaker women frequently appeared as characters in nineteenth-century novels. Yet, despite the regularity with which female Friends were represented in fiction, these characters have received little critical attention. Many of the novels in which they appear have been labeled sentimental and have thus been excluded from the canon of American literature.[3] Even the recent interest in the sentimental novel and the current efforts to recover women's writing have not brought the fictional Quaker women into focus. Perhaps these figures have been ignored because they often appear only briefly in one section of a novel. When they play a larger role, they seem little more than mirror images of such historical Quakers as Mary Dyer, with their words and actions sometimes taken almost verbatim from the chronicles of early American history. On the surface, neither of these characterizations promises fruitful rewards for the literary critic primarily interested in psychological motivation and character development.

Nevertheless, the figure of the Quaker woman *is* important, indeed even central thematically and politically to many of the novels in which she appears. The image of the disruptive Quakeress in Hawthorne's "Gentle Boy" and the literary re-presentations of the historical martyr, Mary Dyer, provide drama in the myriad literary works by authors still fascinated with America's colonial past. More importantly, these persecuted and martyred Quakers, their marginality foregrounded by the treatment they received, also serve as ready analogues for the growing sense among nineteenth-century women of their marginality and political powerlessness. At the very least, the determination, courage, and strength of these Quaker characters provided models of women who could survive in the face of enormous adversity; at best, they showed that women could gain power despite their marginality, albeit in limited areas and at high costs.

More demonstrative of the Quaker woman's literary significance, however, is a second type of character—the Quaker woman, often appearing in a novel only briefly, who offers cultural alternatives inherently subversive to the dominant nineteenth-century ideology of separate spheres. This version of the Quaker character is not the legendary ranting disturber but a quiet, saintly, moral woman, guided by her ethics and convictions rather than by societal norms, who has unusual influence over those around her. By spreading her ethic through the example of her own life, and by revealing to others the moral truth of her positions, the Quaker woman becomes a powerful social force and a subversive figure whose brief appearances in nineteenth-century fiction offer dramatic critiques of dominant cultural norms.

While no direct connection has been documented between Elizabeth Ashbridge and the Quakers in nineteenth-century American novels, her story helps us understand American authors' fascination with the Quaker woman and the way in which they found her useful as a character. Just as Ashbridge used the seventeenth-century Quaker martyrs as models in arriving at self-definition, her own story of abuse and marginalization becomes useful for nineteenth-century women seeking to rationalize their cultural positions and to find sites of power within their own marginalization. Moreover, like the fictional Quaker women, Ashbridge exemplifies the type of principled and moral Quaker woman who influences and transforms others by the quiet strength of her own convictions. For Ashbridge, as for many of the fictional Quaker women in nineteenth-century American fiction, the depth of her beliefs, the consistency between these beliefs and the way in which she led her daily life, and the courage that allowed her to make her principles the final arbiter of her actions came together to give her a formidable presence and, ultimately, the power to affect the behavior of her husband and of people like the young Sarah Stephenson. This kind of moral power, exerted as it was in Ashbridge's case from the margins of society, becomes for several nineteenth-century novelists an alternative vision that allows them a way out of the ideological binds in which their characters find themselves. The Quaker woman character—embodying the heritage of persecution and martyrdom, as well as the unwavering commitment to equality, simplicity, and pacifism inherited from Ashbridge and her eighteenth-century contemporaries—serves as an encoded figure for these novelists. At a time when overt expressions of feminism were suspect and often categorically ignored, the fictional Quaker woman embodied a feminist worldview based on community and family that offered possible solutions for the problems plaguing the dominant culture of nineteenth-century America.

✷

Quaker women dressed in sackcloth, covered with ashes, and seeming slightly mad disrupt Puritan meetings in several novels written during the first half of the nineteenth century. That these fictional descendants of Margaret Brewster, the Massachusetts Quaker who became infamous for similar acts in 1677, along with fictional descendants of the martyred Mary Dyer and of the many nameless women physically abused and expelled from seventeenth-century colonial towns are common figures in American literature two centuries later testifies to the long-lasting cultural resonances of these events. Authors of historical fiction seized on the persecuted Quaker woman as one of a handful of images that simultaneously evoked the authors' fascination with America's colonial past and suggested a parallel between the Quaker critique of New England Puritanism and the burgeoning feminist critique of America in the nineteenth century.

Authors like Rebecca Beach focus their critique of New England by defending its earliest Quaker immigrants. Beach claimed that her novel, *The Puritan and the Quaker: A Story of Colonial Times*, published anonymously in 1879, was occasioned by the marriage of one of her acquaintances to a Quaker woman. Upon bringing his new bride home to "the land which once ordained that Quakers, coming there, should have their tongues burnt through with a hot iron," he and his wife learned that "although the practice was discontinued, the iron of intolerance had not entirely cooled" (iii).[4] To address the ignorance behind this intolerance, Beach corrects historical misinformation about the Quakers by first acknowledging the validity of Puritan complaints against them and then suggesting that Puritan views tell only part of the story:

> It is not to be disputed that the early Quakers brought persecution upon themselves by the aggressiveness of their acts. One is, indeed, driven to sympathize with the grievance of intrusion upon religious worship, and to exult in the punishment of it. But let us remember that this intrusion was not upon their part only. Quakers were dragged from their quiet meetings and thrown into jail, and each attendant found there, was fined or beaten, or both. In short, the government of the Colonies was a despotism, and the Quaker movement, the only persistent protest against it. (iii–iv)

However, Quaker principles, Beach contends, "especially that chief one of liberty of conscience" (v), have triumphed in that they have been embraced by American culture as a whole, and they "will continue to gain ground; while their peculiarities,—no longer called forth by the exigencies of the time,—are fast disappearing before the spirit of enlightened progress" (vii). This prediction hints at the theme, common to several nineteenth-century novels, that Beach makes explicit in the final page of the novel: a lone Quaker figure, possessing personal power, can spread the tenets of Quakerism throughout a community solely through the example of his or her life. For Beach, the early Quakers were in many ways people ahead of their time, and she leaves readers with the reminder of the time "when the Quakers stood alone against abuses that are now cried down by the majority, and if their peculiarities are fast disappearing from our sight, their principles remain" (393).

Other authors, such as John Neal, himself of Quaker parentage, used Quaker figures to batter the Puritans and the mythology sur-rounding them. In *Rachel Dyer: A North American Story* (1828) Neal praises the Puritan fathers as "a ship-load of pious brave men . . . in search of a spot of earth where they might worship their God without fear." However, only a short paragraph later he reminds readers that

> no sooner had these pilgrims touched the shore of the new world, no sooner were they established in comparative power and security, than they fell upon the Quakers, who had followed them over the same sea, with the same hope; and scourged and banished them, and imprisoned them, and put some to death, for not believing as the new church taught in the new world. (35)[5]

For Neal, the Puritans' acts of intolerance held importance beyond their historical time and served to highlight a theme of his novel—the self-perpetuating cyclical uses and abuses of power:

> The persecuted of to-day become the persecutors of to-morrow. They flourish, not because they are right, but because they are per-secuted; and they persecute because they have the power, not because they whom they persecute are wrong. (35)

Neal stopped just short of articulating what his novel implies—that the abuses of power in America's colonial past held lessons for the nineteenth century as well.

The connection between the historical Quakers and contempo-rary nineteenth-century society was made subtly but more explicitly by Eliza Buckminster Lee in *Naomi; or, Boston Two Hundred Years Ago* (1848). The novel opens with the arrival in Boston of Naomi, a nine-teen-year-old woman who has come from England to visit her dying mother, whom she has not seen for ten years. Significantly for the novel's plot, Naomi arrives in a community astir with conversations about evil Quakers who have infiltrated the Puritan community. Naomi, though not herself a Quaker, has been raised since her separa-tion from her mother by a Quaker nurse, Margaret, now her adviser and closest friend.

Throughout the novel's opening, the narrator uses the past tense to set the scene and to provide historical information about the Puritan–Quaker conflict. Only the relatively few details of the plot involving Naomi's debarking from the ship and her entrance to her step father's house are conveyed in the present tense. One striking exception to this pattern, however, is a paragraph on the Quaker belief in the Inner Light. Here the narrator's shift to present tense suggests the passage's relevance to nineteenth-century society:

> The belief, that each individual soul receives light immediately from God himself, has been the spontaneous faith of many of the purest minds throughout the world. Light seems to descend into such minds in periods of darkness, and in the midst of turbulence and oppression. Women, as well as the other sex, pass through deep and earnest struggles after truth. They also wrestle with the angel, and are sometimes victorious. Their natural timidity, forbidding them to publish their thoughts to the world, prevents their struggles and their conquests from being known; but in deep retirement, many live and die in a pure and holy faith, feeling that God is ever near their souls, giving them bread to eat that the world knoweth not of. (31)[6]

The feminist tone in this passage from a novel published in the year of the Seneca Falls Convention is certainly no coincidence. Indeed, much of Lee's text can be read as a struggle among the discourses of nineteenth-century feminism, contemporary political and social movements, and the events described in the novel, set two centuries earlier.

The novels by Beach, Neal, and Lee, as well as numerous others published throughout the nineteenth-century, construct the Puritan past as a parable for the present. For these writers, the parable's lesson is clear: the abuses of power so obvious in the Puritan treatment of Quaker women provide a ready vocabulary with which to encode discourse addressing the social conditions of nineteenth-century women.

These three novels illustrate a pattern in the ways in which nineteenth-century authors used characters meant to evoke but not to replicate historical figures from the seventeenth century. In novels written earlier in the century intricate plot twists customarily connected the heroine to the fictional version of figures from America's past. As the century progressed, however, novelists worked more diligently to separate their protagonists from these quasi-historical figures, arguing instead that their heroines shared few actual similarities with the historical Quakers but instead somehow assimilated only the core of the Quaker ethic. For none of these authors did the fictional versions of historical figures aid in an accurate retelling of history. Instead, these characters, often appearing in historically anachronistic situations, introduced into the novel values and beliefs that influenced the Quaker (or quasi-Quaker) heroines and against which the heroines were judged. Almost without exception, the historical figures after whom these characters were roughly patterned lived outside the dominant Puritan culture, often as victims of persecution. In addition to Margaret Brewster and Mary Dyer, stock figures in nineteenth-century novels include Anne Hutchinson, women accused of practicing witchcraft in Salem in 1692, and Native Americans. The number of characters victimized by the Puritans in any one novel is sometimes overwhelming, leaving readers with entire catalogs of the Puritan fathers' sins. In each case, the woman at the center of the novel feels some particular bond or sense of community with the "others" who are also thrust away from the dominant culture.

Neal's *Rachel Dyer* exemplifies the novel that posits direct links between the main protagonist and a historical ancestor—in this case, Mary Dyer. In Neal's novel loosely historicized characters abound in a confusing array of anachronistic situations. Among his cast are most of the participants in the Salem witchcraft trials—accused and accusers with slightly altered but still recognizable names, the infamous Quaker martyrs, and Anne Hutchinson, here renamed Elizabeth Hutchinson. Indeed, even the action of the novel is a jumble of partially reworked passages from the witchcraft trial transcripts.

To expose the injustices of New England's past, Neal intertwines the early Quakers' martyrdom with the persecution of those accused of witchcraft, suggesting an ongoing cycle of abuses from which there is little hope of escape. In the novel, the women on trial for witchcraft have presumably been accused because they scoffed at Mary Dyer, the "aged woman of the Quakers," on the occasion of her martyrdom; the accused witches who were later put to death on the site of Dyer's death included the daughter of one of Dyer's judges (36–37). Neal's readers could only assume that this seemingly unending cycle—the persecuted turning persecutor—could be traced back to the treatment received by the earliest Puritans in England, and that the cycle would remain uninterrupted until the societal power dynamics were radically altered.

At the center of this cycle of persecutions, Neal places the title character, Rachel Dyer, the deformed granddaughter of the infamous martyr Mary Dyer. A Quaker herself, Rachel is haunted by her grandmother's reputation, and her actions are constantly guided by that heritage:

> having been very familiar with the aspect of peril from her youth, and being aware that she was looked up to with awe by the multitude—not so much with fear, as with a religious awe—great love mingled with a secret, mysterious veneration, as the chief hope of her grandmother, Mary Dyer, the prophetess and the martyr— she determined to play for that stake. (199)

Described in terms befitting her grandmother, Rachel is a Quaker woman "of tried worth and remarkable courage" (199) "who spoke out with a voice of authority" (147) and whose "holy regard for truth" made her "simple asseveration of more value than the oath of most people" (147–48). Given this heritage, it is no surprise that in the large crowd Rachel's is the only voice raised in protest as Sarah Good, named as a witch, is hauled off in a cart to her death. True to his theory that those in positions of authority "persecute because they have the power, not because they whom they persecute are wrong" (35), Neal makes Rachel's outspoken criticism of the Puritan persecutors lead to her own downfall.

Rachel herself is soon accused of witchcraft by a woman against whom she testified in an attempt to save yet another innocent victim of the witchcraft hysteria. Although testifying against this woman jeopardizes her own life, Rachel is driven to tell what she knows to be the truth under the weight of her grandmother's moral commitment to do what is right. She is, of course, sentenced to death and thus becomes another victim of the cycle of persecution. Although on the eve of her scheduled execution she dies of natural causes with a smile on her face and her arm around the Bible (263), thereby robbing her tormenters of the satisfaction of taking her life, she can hardly be viewed as a woman who is triumphant against the system. In a description of Rachel as she stands awaiting trial, however, Neal does suggest a victory of sorts:

> —Rachel standing up as it were with a new stature—up, with her forehead flashing to the sky and her coarse red hair shining and shivering about her huge head with a frightful fixed gleam,—her cap off, her cloak thrown aside and her distorted shape, for the first time, in full view of the awe-struck multitude . . . It was Rachel Dyer—the red-haired witch—the freckled witch—the hump-backed witch they saw now—but they saw not her ugliness, they saw not that she was either unshapely or unfair. They saw only that she was brave. They saw that although she was a woman upon the very threshold of eternity, she was not afraid of the aspect of death. (226)

Radiant with the courage of her convictions, her manner outshines and even masks her physical deformities and moves her into the ranks of the early Quaker martyrs, even though it is not her religious beliefs specifically that are on trial. In this final shining public moment, Neal hints at Rachel's ability to prefigure the kind of life—a quiet and moral Quaker life—that could undergird a society capable of breaking the vicious cycle of persecution. His note of hope, however, is muted if not silenced by Rachel's death and, through her, the symbolic extinguishing of her grandmother's spirit.

Like Neal, Lee employs a gallery of fictionalized re-presentations of historical figures. If Lee's *Naomi* is less confused than Neal's *Rachel Dyer* by anachronisms, the novel is still the site of continual conflict between Lee's efforts simultaneously to link Naomi with historic figures and to separate her from them. This conflict goes beyond Lee's attempt to render faithfully both Puritan and Quaker beliefs and actions, "to preserve," as she notes in her preface, "as much as was in my power, an exact justice between the two parties" (iii). The confusion for Lee results from her yoking the discourse of nineteenth-century gender ideology to the Quaker beliefs expounded by the title character, Naomi Worthington, a young woman coming to terms with her own commitment to Quakerism. Despite the confusion this connection causes in the novel, the conflicts Naomi faces strikingly illustrate the usefulness of the Quaker woman in exploring the ideological bind that trapped many women in the mid-nineteenth century.

Naomi's "transparent features" reflect "the full assurance of perfect truth" and signify "one of those pure poetical souls, that had as yet found no manifestation" (29). Naomi's separation from her mother has left that solitary poetical soul unfulfilled and frustrated:

> But her young heart thirsted for excellence; she yearned for an unknown, but a possible, goodness, which she found not around her,—neither in nature nor in the world, neither in the church nor in society, neither in sermons nor in books. The conception of this ideal goodness was ever before her: but she found it not in herself, and wept that she was never nearer to it than to the rainbow in the horizon. (30–31)

This pattern of solitude and searching, similar to what Ashbridge experienced, positions Naomi as a perfect candidate for the Quaker Inner Light. Furthermore, Naomi's connection to Margaret—her Quaker nurse, foster mother, and confidant—has already provided her with a grounding in the Quaker ethic, although Naomi is not officially a member of that faith.

Because Naomi's American stepfather detests the Society of Friends, however, Margaret has remained temporarily in England. Naomi thus feels alone:

> alone in the world and alone in her religious faith,—for she could not sympathize or mingle with those who professed the same faith that she believed, and the faith of the Puritans repelled all the sympathies of her soul. (75)

Lacking sympathy for the Puritans, Naomi is most comfortable among those living outside of Boston's dominant culture in an Indian village—"the most purely congenial scene she had witnessed in New England" (96). She lives there with her mother's servant girl, Faith, and the family's black slave, Sambo. Later in the novel, Naomi takes refuge in the "witch's cabin" (197) of an Indian medicine woman whose language she finds "so unaffectedly simple and expressive . . . that it affected Naomi more than the most artfully wrought tale" (207).

Despite Naomi's resolve to keep her Quaker sympathies hidden, the material manifestations of her belief make it difficult. Although Naomi is appalled and fearful when she witnesses the Quaker woman in sackcloth and ashes interrupting the Puritan meeting (53–54), "the simplicity of her own dress was the subject of excessive and almost incredulous surprise" among members of the same Puritan congregation (64). A young man in the congregation suspects Naomi of Quakerism because of her dress and "a certain composed air" (68). He thus finds her slightly subversive:

> To be sure you do not say *thee* and *thou*, and you go to [Puritan] meeting; but you know there are many who do not disapprove some of the tenets of the Quakers, and though these do not come out openly in their favor, and do not avow their own sentiments, they seem to me like wolves in sheep's clothing. (68)

That the implied threat here is not based solely on theological differences is evident in an earlier narrative juxtaposition of Naomi's Quaker sympathies with Anne Hutchinson's beliefs. Immediately following a discussion about the Quaker Inner Light being equally accessible to both women and men, the narrator recounts the story of Hutchinson, suggesting her inevitable connection to Quaker women empowered by the Inner Light and the Quaker commitment to equality. Noting that "Mrs. Hutchinson had broken through the restraints of sex, and exhibited in this country her masculine and independent spirit," the narrator feels "obliged to admit that [Hutchinson's] martyrdom (for it was no less) was as much the fruit of her inordinate self-esteem as of her intellectual superiority over others." Further, the narrator fears that when Hutchinson examined her life, "she must have feared that the slimy trail of spiritual pride had sullied the white robes of her martyrdom" (31–32). In contrast to Hutchinson's "masculine" spirit, young "Naomi was too truly a woman, and from instinctive delicacy knew too well the position she held, ever to have made the struggles of her soul the theme of public discussion" (32). Naomi does not disclose her Quaker sympathies because "she felt no call for martyrdom, nor even for persecution." She also knows that in "secret and silent worship of the heart, she could offend neither church nor state" (38).

More important than Naomi's actions, however, is the passage's obvious association of Quakerism with the gender roles ingrained in nineteenth-century society. Hutchinson's "independent spirit" and the "inordinate self-esteem" that prompted her to speak publicly to an audience—which included "the Puritan saint, Cotton, [who] himself

would have been her disciple" (31) had she continued to hold her
meetings—are labeled "masculine" traits; conversely, Naomi's "instinctive delicacy," her awareness of "the position she held," and her willingness to forego "public discussion" for the "secret and silent worship
of the heart" mark her as "truly a woman," a designation that promised
to spare her from Hutchinson's fate. That Naomi's sense of delicacy is
"instinctive" rather than learned suggests that Quakerism somehow
runs against nature as well as against culturally sanctioned gender roles.

If the gender lines and the sins of Hutchinson and the Quakers
in crossing them seem clear in the novel's opening pages, they are
hopelessly muddled in its later passages. Midway through the novel,
Naomi contemplates how best to aid her friend, Margaret, who,
having arrived in the colonies, "began to use the intemperate language
of the Quakers," was arrested and sentenced to be whipped out of
Boston "and then to have her tongue bored with a red-hot iron" (165).
Guided by her own sense of duty and by love for her foster mother
and friend, Naomi resolves to help Margaret escape. The narrator
presents Naomi's willingness to act on Margaret's behalf and her
inherent ability in actualizing her goals as challenges to nineteenth-
century gender stereotypes:

> Naomi, in union with the feminine gentleness of her character, pos-
> sessed a courageous, an almost lion-hearted independence in the
> cause of humanity, and where the service of those she loved was
> involved, no effort seemed beyond her power. (166)

The "independence" earlier associated with Hutchinson's downfall
here becomes an asset for Naomi. Combined with her "feminine gentleness," it suggests that the culturally sanctioned boundaries between
feminine and masculine traits are at least partially permeable. Lee carries this suggestion even farther when Naomi develops a plan to bribe
Margaret's jailer and to help her escape. The plan becomes evidence of
what the narrator views as women's innate superiority:

> This plan may seem Quixotic and wholly improbable to my readers,
> but women have often succeeded in enterprises so dangerous or
> delicate that men have shrunk from attempting them. (168)

The strength of even this brief moment of female empowerment is
diluted, however, as Naomi recognizes a parallel between the Quaker

women who were to be whipped out of town and the pair of yoked oxen who would pull the cart to which they would be attached:

> The honest, stolid, but mild and even humane countenances of the oxen intimated no sympathy with the inhuman preparations going on under their very breath. One of them had laid himself down, patiently ruminating and chewing the sweet morsel, while he drew the head of the other down uncomfortably towards him; even in these patient, submissive creatures intimating the supremacy of the one over the free-will of the other. (168)

Does Naomi's observation suggest her awareness of the dominant Puritan culture's effect on what she perceives as the inherent truth in Quaker practices? Is it a protofeminist recognition of patriarchal oppression of all women? Or does it simply foreshadow Naomi's downfall resulting from her decision to aid Margaret?

The rescue plan succeeds when Margaret is disguised in Naomi's cloak and sent off on Naomi's horse. This substitution of one woman for the other symbolically transforms Naomi into a Quaker and reifies what Naomi has privately known about herself for a long time. As this substitution provides a thematic triumph in revealing Naomi's heretofore concealed sentiments, it also marks the novel's retreat from any assertion of a feminist agenda underlying Naomi's newly announced Quakerism. Her now public complicity with Margaret seals Naomi's fate and begins the series of events leading inevitably to her arrest. At her trial, patterned almost directly after Anne Hutchinson's, Naomi is found guilty and, like Hutchinson, banished from the colony.[7]

Lee's decision to model Naomi's trial on Hutchinson's would at first suggest some parallel between Hutchinson's well-documented challenge to the colony's patriarchal leadership and Naomi's own response to her accusers. However, Lee's use of this historical precedent confuses more than it clarifies—particularly since earlier efforts to distance Naomi from Hutchinson's masculine independence are further reinforced in the trial scene. Perhaps recalling Hutchinson's fatal mistake and determining not to make a similar one, Naomi initially asserts herself in front of the magistrates by refusing to answer their questions about her religious beliefs. Her resolve is lost, however, when she is told that she will also be tried in a church court:

A gulf was suddenly opened before her, from which there was no escape. The other offence, prompted by gratitude and humanity, would be excused by every benevolent heart, and if punished as a violation of a recent law, could be punished only very lightly; but to think for herself upon great questions, to dare to differ from her spiritual teachers, to dare to hold opinions at variance with the only true church, was the unpardonable sin of the age, stigmatized as blasphemy, a sin for whose forgiveness the angels might plead in vain. (286–87)

With this catalog of fears, the narrator irreparably severs the connection between Naomi and the more confident Hutchinson. Rejecting any vestiges of independence, Naomi submits to patriarchal authority. More confusing is Lee's implication that Naomi does so because she sees the possibility of a "benevolent heart" and light punishment in the same Puritan culture that only recently offered her no source of comfort or support. One can only wonder at Naomi's supposed concern for the dictates of "the only true church" and her obligations to the ministers of that church.

Even the courageous heritage of the Quaker martyrs cannot guide Naomi through her crisis, for Lee takes pains to distance Naomi from any links to these historical figures as well:

Naomi, although she differed altogether from the orthodox church, held nothing in common with the Quakers of that day but the essential principle of their faith, the belief of the inward voice of truth in the soul; this she held above all other inspiration,—to be obeyed and honored as the voice of God,—obeyed rather than the authority of any church, were it the church of the bishops, or the church of the elders. She adopted none of the peculiarities of the Quakers; she *thee-d* and *thou-ed* no one. Her dress differed only from the reigning fashion by its more tasteful simplicity. (243)

The contradiction between the above passage and the church court passage is obvious. If Naomi retains "the essential principle" of Quakerism, her fear of holding "opinions at variance" with the Puritan church makes no sense. Certainly her continued antinomian belief in "the inward voice of truth in the soul," acknowledged publicly through her actions to save Margaret, holds strong affinity with Quaker teachings. Instead of demonstrating the kind of courage and strength that later comes to be associated with Quaker women in literature, however, Naomi loses heart and defers to the patriarchal system she faces. "[T]oo truly a woman" to survive the ordeal she faces, she perishes—not physically like Rachel Dyer, but spiritually as she is banished from the colony.

Finding coherence in Lee's characterization of Naomi, a confusing task, is possible only by understanding a connection between the seventeenth-century story line and the nineteenth-century ideologies of gender that were under attack by the burgeoning feminist movement, even as Lee wrote her novel. By linking Naomi both to the traditions of Hutchinson's antinomianism and to Quakerism, Lee appears in the first part of the novel to suggest that Naomi, like her historical ancestors, embodies the ability to challenge and even to subvert the patriarchal system around her while still seeming to be governed by a "feminine gentleness of character" that made her aware of her proper social position. However, as the last part of the novel shows, Naomi fails at subversion and is even more firmly entrenched in the dominant ideology at the end of the novel than she is at its beginning. As long as Naomi conceals her Quakerism, she is allowed a certain subversive power among those who mistake her for one of their own. She can act on her hidden belief in equality that allows her to blur the lines between gendered spheres, acting when necessary with the "masculine" independence and courage that allows her to save her friend. Only when her Quaker sympathies become public does she lose her pretense of "true womanhood" by her acknowledged belief in a doctrine that takes equality as a given. Naomi thereby becomes a potent threat to the very foundations of nineteenth-century ideology and must save herself solely within the masculine realm that requires independence of thought and the courage to challenge the magistrates' authority. Naomi fails because, as the narrator explains early in the novel, she "from instinctive delicacy knew too well the position she held, ever to have made the struggles of her soul the theme of public discussion" (32). The instinct that prevents public discussion also prevents public defense. Lee's characterization of Naomi suggests that any woman operating within the constructed ideology of separate spheres is unlikely to subvert it.

In *The Puritan and the Quaker: A Story of Colonial Times,* Rebecca
Beach presents a young heroine who, like Naomi, has strong ties to
Quakerism but is not technically a member of the Quaker meeting.
Unlike Naomi, however, Beach's Edith Morrison is neither conflicted
nor destroyed by her insider-outsider status. She survives by living
according to a Quaker ethic while demonstrating to non-Quakers the
validity of her principles. Even at her young age, she has learned that
"there is but a step between enthusiasm and fanaticism" (28), and she
has anchored herself a safe distance away from that dangerous cultural
precipice. Owing in large part to Edith's cultural position, Beach's text
has subversive potential. The novel embraces Quakerism's basic principles and shows, through the author's depiction of Edith, that these
principles in their less fanatical permutations are not only compatible
with those of the dominant culture but also have influenced nineteenth-
century social and religious thought:

> No doubt we should find to-day, were the truth known, that popu-
> lar and enlightened views upon religious subjects approach the stan-
> dards of the early Quakers rather than that of the Puritans. (393)

At first glance, young Edith Morrison seems a paragon of the nineteenth-century ideal of true womanhood. Among the small group of
Quakers gathering secretly to worship in Boston, Edith, with an
expression and demeanor softer than that of the men around her,
directs all her energies and attention to the safety and comfort of her
father, who in turn is most concerned about his daughter's safety.
Although she has adopted the plain style of dress, "the homely
fashion of her Quaker garb could not conceal that she was beautiful
and pleasant to the eye" (10). Only a few pages into the novel, however, it becomes clear that Edith is not a passive woman. Although
not a Quaker herself, she has absorbed the faith's principles from her
Quaker father and has chosen to live her life accordingly. She has also
internalized the model of Quaker women challenging authority in
support of their beliefs. Despite her impending persecution and
imprisonment, Edith insists on remaining with her father even though
he orders her away from him, arguing that she need not endure punishment for Quaker beliefs when technically she is not a Quaker. She
would, he argues, be safer if she would count herself among the ene-

mies of the Quakers. The blending of Quaker beliefs and nineteenth-century gender stereotypes is evident in their exchange:

> "I will go with thee even unto death, but never, no, never, will I profess their blood-stained faith."
>
> "Thou speakest in too violent a tone; thy words are not in the meek spirit of humility. A more submissive condition of mind better fitteth thine age and duty to thy parent. Prepare, then, I say, to leave this place ere sunrise of to-morrow, with one who offers thee protection, for, alas, I can afford thee none!"
>
> "Thou shalt not send me from thee, father. In all else thou mayest claim obedience, but never will I consent to leave thee, nor does the duty of a child extend so far." (12)

As this passage indicates, the Quaker sense of duty and the Quaker abhorrence of violence intermingle with the discourse of gender, making the sense of duty Edith feels to her father a "submissive condition" and her strong assertion of her intention to fulfill that duty an act of violence that her father later labels "unwomanly" (13). Similarly, when her father is jailed for his beliefs, Edith visits Governor Endicott to plead either for her father's freedom or for the right to be incarcerated with him, an act that once again demonstrates both her courage and her willingness to enter the public arena in support of her convictions. The governor is aghast at such audacity in a woman: "There is witchcraft among these Quakers, surely, for even their sucking babes possess this indomitable spirit!" (169–70). The extent to which Edith would go to fulfill her duty to her father, along with her outspoken defense of this responsibility, mark her as extraordinary in Beach's fictional representation of Puritan Boston.

The governor's immediate and seemingly instinctive connection between his perception of Edith's difference and the practice of witchcraft highlights the ideological association of the Quakers with other marginal figures of seventeenth-century New England society, particularly those accused of practicing witchcraft. The connection between Edith and others living outside the dominant culture is reinforced when Edith befriends Maretah, a Native American woman:

> A warm mutual affection soon sprung up and strengthened between these two young women; the one, a fair type of the culture

of the old world, the other, of the natural freedom of the new, and each finding in her opposite, points of mutual attraction, and a common ground of dependence and sympathy. (205)

Edith's marginalization becomes literal as well as symbolic when she and her father, upon his eventual release from prison, are forced to live on the outskirts of the town, isolated from the rest of the community. Reminiscent of Hester Prynne's separation from the Puritan culture around her, the displacement of these Quakers to the geographical margins of society highlights the fear of their influence, a fear that recognizes the potentially seductive power of their teachings for non-Quakers.

Edith ultimately proves that the fears of the community's magistrates are well-founded. Although she is officially a member of the Church of England, her commitment to the tenets of Quakerism is complete. Not only does she adopt the testimonies of simplicity and equality, but she is also linked, through her suitor, William Robinson, to the infamous trio of Quaker martyrs—Robinson, Marmaduke Stephenson, and Mary Dyer—whose executions are retold as part of the novel's plot (222–27). Yet even with this direct connection to the most fanatical of the Quaker characters, young Edith has no trouble finding allies outside the meeting when, after her father's death, she is arrested for her beliefs. Most spectacular among her long list of advocates is Mr. Harding, "one of the chief magistrates of the town" and "among the most bitter enemies of the Quakers" (14). When Edith reveals to him that she is not nor has she ever been an official member of the Society of Friends, his attitude toward her suddenly changes, and he pleads her case before Governor Endicott:

> If you are really determined to send her to prison, you shall send us thither in company, for I declare that if *she* has been guilty of contempt (which she disclaims) then I have been equally culpable; for in naught that she hath said have I discovered any thing to condemn, or that I do not entirely coincide in. (307)

Harding's defense is proof of Edith's subversive power. Not only does this defense illustrate the Quaker's power to influence those around him or her, but it also foregrounds the extent to which Quaker principles and ideals, when divorced from the Quaker label, seem eminently reasonable to non-Quakers and mesh almost imperceptibly with the best of the dominant ideology.

By remaining a member of the dominant culture—albeit in name only—while practicing and spreading the tenets of Quakerism, Edith becomes a highly subversive figure. Surviving in a culture overtly hostile to her beliefs, she has accomplished what Naomi Worthington could not. By avoiding fanaticism, which in this context means also avoiding membership in the Society of Friends, she earns respect for her views and wins converts to her positions, even though her actions to support those beliefs challenge cultural norms of femininity at every turn. As the narrator explains:

> [The Quakers'] consistent purity of life and unshrinking obedience to the voice of conscience, won her reverence, and she was able to do justice to their religious profession, even while deploring that exaggerated view of duty that sometimes led them into extravagances which their warmest friends could scarcely excuse.
>
> True to her father's teaching, no fear of man ever turned her from her duty, and others, taking courage from her example, began to walk fearlessly in the plain path before them. Her husband and Mr. Harding never ceased to interpose in behalf of the Quakers when opportunity called upon them to do so, and the former lived to rejoice in the day when persecution ceased and this peculiar people settled down into quiet and useful members of society. (389–90)

This peaceful vision clearly reveals the limits of Edith's subversive powers. While she retains her power to affect others' beliefs, she does so only by achieving higher standing in the dominant culture around her than she held at the novel's outset. By the end of the story, Edith has married a non-Quaker who, along with Mr. Harding, intercedes on her behalf, whereas in the beginning it was Edith who interceded for others. Edith survives because she dampens the intensity with which she adheres to her principles. If her husband "lived to rejoice in the day when persecution ceased," he rejoiced for a Quaker people who have been silenced and have lost their peculiarity by blending into the culture around them. Through the final vision of Edith's life, Beach argues for compromise and conciliation, and she, like Lee, ultimately must retreat from any overt call to subversion.

Rachel Dyer, Naomi Worthington, and Edith Morrison are three very different characters in equally diverse novels, but they share something beyond Quaker sympathies and the seventeenth-century settings in which they appear. All three challenge the dominant patriarchal system that paralleled the system within which the authors of these novels wrote. All three are ultimately beaten by that system— Rachel Dyer dies; Naomi is banished; and Edith is absorbed into the system, thereby losing much of the power she was able to wield from the outside.

✳

Not all Quaker women in nineteenth-century American novels are thwarted in their efforts. Several novels from the last half of the century introduce Quaker women who inherit the sense of ethics, morality, and courage of their historical ancestors, even though these early Quaker martyrs are not mentioned. Unlike the protagonists of the historical novels discussed above, these later heroines live squarely within the nineteenth century, where they both shape and are shaped by the concerns of contemporary culture. These quiet, saintly women, who typically appear only briefly in compressed scenes, model an alternative cultural order and a corrective vision that addresses the ills of contemporary society and critiques the nineteenth-century rhetoric of individualism. Founded on Quaker testimonies of simplicity and equality, the ethos conveyed by these characters is emphatically communal. Works as varied as Harriet Beecher Stowe's *Uncle Tom's Cabin; or, Life among the Lowly* (1852), Rebecca Harding Davis's *Life in the Iron Mills* (1861), and Louisa May Alcott's *Work: A Story of Experience* (1873) contrast the dominant model of competitive individualism with a Quaker woman who quietly demonstrates a cooperative, egalitarian, and largely domestic ethic, more attractive than cut-throat competition and—the reader is led to hope—ultimately more viable as public policy.

In *Uncle Tom's Cabin* Rachel Halliday is the prototypical Quaker mother, a woman of "fifty-five or sixty" with "just the face and form that made 'mother' seem the most natural word in the world" for her (215–16).[8] Her attire immediately bespeaks her spiritual affiliation:

> The snowy lisse crape cap, made after the strait Quaker pattern,—
> the plain white muslin handkerchief, lying in placid folds across her
> bosom,—the drab shawl and dress,—showed at once the commu-
> nity to which she belonged. (215)

Furthermore, Rachel's favorite rocking chair identifies her position
within the family:

> It had a turn for quacking and squeaking,—that chair had,—either
> from having taken cold in early life, or from some asthmatic affec-
> tion, or perhaps from nervous derangement; but, as she gently
> swung backward and forward, the chair kept up a kind of subdued
> "creechy crawchy," that would have been intolerable in any other
> chair. . . . [F]or twenty years or more, nothing but loving words, and
> gentle moralities, and motherly loving kindness, had come from
> that chair;—head-aches and heart-aches innumerable had been
> cured there,—difficulties spiritual and temporal solved there,—
> all by one good, loving woman. (215–16)

In just one brief chapter Stowe describes Rachel in terms redolent of
her power and prestige within the Quaker settlement, a community
that revolves almost exclusively around "the quiet scene" of Rachel's
kitchen. "Large, roomy, neatly-painted . . . without a particle of dust,"
it is filled with "rows of shining tin, suggestive of unmentionable good
things to the appetite," and with Quaker friends who seem as much at
home there as do Rachel and her husband Simeon (214). Like Rachel
herself, the kitchen exudes a clean, quiet, and ordered demeanor that
draws her family and the entire community into its embrace:

> Everything went on so sociably, so quietly, so harmoniously, in the
> great kitchen,—it seemed so pleasant to every one to do just what
> they were doing, there was such an atmosphere of mutual confi-
> dence and good fellowship everywhere,—even the knives and forks
> had a social clatter as they went on to the table. (223)

Rachel is unquestionably the architect and guardian of that harmony.
Simeon, illustrating the operative principles of collectivity and cooperation, takes his place next to Rachel, sifting meal for corncakes while
Rachel makes biscuits and prepares chicken (222). The greatest activity
and energy within the kitchen comes from Rachel and from Ruth, her

young Quaker counterpart. Simeon willingly allows Rachel center stage, as he stands "before a little looking-glass in the corner, engaged in the antipatriarchal operation of shaving" while she presides over the preparations for the meal (223). With dialogue and action showing him as an integral part of the family unit, this scene can be read as assent to the woman-centered events that he observes, an approval governed by his commitment to Quaker egalitarianism.[9]

Although the image of Rachel in the kitchen fits easily into the nineteenth-century image of a woman in her proper sphere, it also unsettles cultural ideologies of gender even as it appears to enforce them. Rachel's authority over the meal has importance beyond the domestic sphere of her home. Looking "so truly and benignly happy . . . at the head of the table," she presides over a meal celebrating the reunion of the fugitive slave family: Eliza, George, and baby Harry (223). Moreover, this breakfast has even greater political significance: it marks "the first time that ever George had sat down on equal terms at any white man's table" (223).

In this tangible enactment of the Quaker commitment to equality, Stowe represents the efficacy of the Quaker principles in operation. That these principles are radical is clear in the sharp contrast between the peace and quiet harmony reigning in Rachel's kitchen and the frenzied tension of much of the rest of the novel's world, where families are wrenched apart, danger is always imminent, and fear of capture provides constant drama. The starkness of this disparity intensifies the implicit message of Stowe's depiction of the Quaker settlement. Framed by the viciousness and inhumanity of slave trading, the scene in the Quaker village speaks with a quietness that is extraordinarily powerful in comparison to the outer world. The Halliday home and, by extension, the entire Quaker settlement functions on principles of simplicity, equality, and pacifism deemed threatening by the dominant culture; yet within the context for this scene, these principles can only appear as sane alternatives to the chaos in almost every non-Quaker setting. Through the juxtaposition she creates, Stowe forces readers to rethink questions about cultural stability and the stereotypic Quaker role in disrupting that stability. In this novel, only the Quakers are able to maintain any degree of familial and communal cohesiveness amid the chaos and tragedy surrounding them.

The Quaker values of the Halliday home provide the only real
hope for change in *Uncle Tom's Cabin*. Within the immaculate cleanliness of Rachel's kitchen and the "good fellowship and mutual confidence" among the people who occupy it, the brutality of the slave
trade has no place. Here an ethic of racial equality allows Eliza to feel
as much at home in one of the rocking chairs, "gently swaying back
and forward, her eyes bent on some fine sewing," as does Rachel in the
other (214); here George can overcome his "constraint and awkward-
ness" with white people because he is warmed by "the genial morning
rays of this simple, overflowing kindness" (223). Rachel, the sun from
whom these genial rays emanate, has established an egalitarian spirit
within her home that makes the reunion of the fugitive slave family as
important as is the harmony within her own. Yet, as Philip Fisher and
others have noted, this scene of reconciliation and racial harmony is
dreamlike, a temporary delusion that cannot last (110–11). Eliza's dream
of "a beautiful country" highlights the correlation between dreams and
the transitoriness of their stay at the Halliday home:

> [T]here, in a house which kind voices told her was a home, she saw
> her boy playing, free and happy child. She heard her husband's
> footsteps; she felt him coming nearer; his arms were around her, his
> tears falling on her face, and she awoke! It was no dream. The day-
> light had long faded; her child lay calmly sleeping by her side; a
> candle was burning dimly on the stand, and her husband was sob-
> bing by her pillow. (222)

Like Eliza's dream, the idyllic vision of the reunited slave family eating
at the table of white folks blurs fantasy and reality, and it fades quickly
once George and Eliza leave the relative safety of the Quaker settlement. By the end of the chapter, the realities of danger and flight creep
into the tranquility of the Quaker village as Simeon tells George of
the plans for the next stage of their journey. They must leave that
night, for "the pursuers are hard after thee; we must not delay" (225).
As if to emphasize the fleetingness of racial harmony, Stowe intro-
duces this reminder of the slave trade into the one place in the novel
that is antithetical to it.

The edenic vision of racial harmony is brief in the context of
nineteenth-century cultural politics. Ultimately, neither Rachel nor

Simeon, nor even the entire Quaker settlement, can end the brutalities of the slave trade. Although they admirably put into practice their abolitionist beliefs, these Friends can offer only a temporary respite to those few fugitive slaves who arrive on their doorstep. However welcome and efficacious this aid may be for the fortunate few, it cannot eliminate or correct the horrors of slavery that Stowe excoriates in her novel.

However, even if Stowe's Quaker community cannot provide a satisfactory corrective to slavery's evils, it posits a solution to rugged individualism, another issue of contention within nineteenth-century American culture. Although the novel implicitly critiques the idealism of Rachel's kitchen in so far as that scene pertains to the issue of slavery, it also offers a vision of a successful community governed by the principles of equality, simplicity, and pacifism. With these beliefs at its core, the Quaker settlement prophesies a successful society operating on an ethic of cooperation and collectivity rather than on a model of competitive individualism. What is truly radical in Stowe's vision has less to do with her thematic focus on slavery than with her vision of a domestic cultural system based upon a cooperative theory of labor, in which a Quaker woman gently but firmly controls the terms of the collectivity to ensure the efficient functioning of her home. All those at work in the kitchen "moved obediently to Rachel's gentle 'Thee had better,' or more gentle, 'Hadn't thee better?' in the work of getting breakfast;" and "if there was any danger of friction or collision from the ill-regulated zeal of so many young operators, her gentle 'Come! come!' or 'I wouldn't now,' was quite sufficient to allay the difficulty" (222–23). In her position of quiet power within the successful community, Rachel subverts the dominant nineteenth-century gender ideology of separate spheres, for her kitchen is at once the perfect example of domesticity and the site of contentious actions relating to the most hotly debated of contemporary public issues. Rachel's role in both the public and the private spheres works to dismantle the very foundation of nineteenth-century ideology. Furthermore, to avoid any confusion about the practicality of Rachel's methods, the narrator offers the following assessment of the usefulness of her model to contemporary culture:

> Bards have written of the cestus of Venus, that turned the heads of all the world in successive generations. We had rather, for our part,

have the cestus of Rachel Halliday, that kept heads from being
turned, and made everything go on harmoniously. We think it is
more suited to our modern days, decidedly. (223)

Thus, Rachel's placid tranquility as she defines the terms of her community makes her an admirable and useful model for American culture at midcentury.

Less than ten years later, another Quaker woman sharing many
of Rachel's characteristics appears in Rebecca Harding Davis's *Life in
the Iron Mills*. Like Rachel, this nameless Quaker is notable for her
simplicity and quiet demeanor. She is "a homely body, coarsely dressed
in gray and white," distinguished by her Quaker silence: "Of all the
crowd there that day, this woman alone had not spoken . . ." (61).[10] But
no one mistakes her silence for timidity: "[T]here was no meekness, or
sorrow, in her face; the stuff out of which murderers are made, instead"
(61). From her first appearance, this nameless woman, like Rachel
Halliday, exudes a quiet competence in the pursuit of what she understands to be her duty to fellow human beings.

The arena in which this woman performs her duties could not be
farther from Rachel's domestic paradise. Davis's Quaker has left the
domestic sphere to work in the industrial world dominated by the filth
of the iron mills. The oppressive and inescapable dirt from the mills
that characterizes the entire town graphically illustrates the ills of the
industrialization that caused it.

> The sky sank down before dawn, muddy, flat, immovable. The air is
> thick, clammy with the breath of crowded human beings. . . .
>   The idiosyncrasy of this town is smoke. It rolls sullenly in slow
> folds from the great chimneys of the iron-foundries, and settles
> down in black, slimy pools on the muddy streets. Smoke on the
> wharves, smoke on the dingy boats, on the yellow river,—clinging
> in a coating of greasy soot to the house-front, the two faded
> poplars, the faces of the passers-by. (11)

Within this stifling and depressing atmosphere, the Quaker appears in
the most stifling and horrible place—the prison. Brought into the
novel only in its final pages, this saintly woman arrives at the jail just
after the protagonist, Hugh Wolfe, commits suicide. A furnace tender

in the iron mill who has been convicted of larceny, Wolfe has received a nineteen-year sentence and, in despair over his condition and unable to endure the inhumane brutality of prison life, he ends his life. His suicide causes a crowd to gather in his cell, with everyone from the coroner to newspaper editors to young boys "with their hands thrust knowingly into their pockets and heads on one side" squeezing in to gawk at the dead man. The only women amidst this crowd are the Quaker, "sitting on the end of the pallet, holding [Wolfe's] head in her arms—with the ferocity of a watch-dog, if any of them touched the body," and Deborah, Wolfe's cousin and a prisoner from the adjacent cell (61).

Davis's decision to include a Quaker woman in her story in the prison scene is not surprising, since Quaker women were at the forefront of nineteenth-century prison-reform movements. However, Davis provides abundant clues that her purpose in introducing this character goes far beyond mere historical veracity. As the Quaker gently tends Hugh Wolfe's body, she

> in the same still, gentle way, brought a vase of wood-leaves and berries, and placed it by the pallet, then opened the narrow window. The fresh air blew in, and swept the woody fragrance over the dead face. (61–62)

Like the fresh air wafting through the open window, the Quaker herself is a welcome change in the stifling atmosphere of the prison cell and in the palpable heaviness of the dismal town. By recognizing Hugh's human needs, she does for him what no other character in the novel can do. Laying out his body, the Quaker woman ignores or perhaps even fails to notice the ignobility that has allowed the rest of the townspeople to shun him and force him into the predicament that ultimately precipitates his suicide.

The woman's sense of duty to Hugh stands in marked contrast to the overt denial of responsibility that systematically is asserted by every other character. Even Doctor May rejects any obligation he has to help Hugh, though earlier he stands out from the other townspeople by recognizing the poignancy of the Korl Woman, a statue that Wolfe has carved out of the refuse from the smelted iron. Although May, with a background in traditional Christianity, once understood that "much good was to be done" for Hugh "by a friendly word or two: a latent genius to be warmed into life by a waited-for sun-beam" (36–37), he still cannot bring himself to sacrifice his elevated class position in order to give the man the help he needs. To abdicate his responsibility, May symbolically washes himself when he is haunted by the memory of Wolfe's sculpture touching his soul (45). When Wolfe is arrested, May immediately forgets the neediness he once recognized in Hugh and remembers only that for one brief moment he had bestowed from his elevated position a word of beneficent kindness on the lowly mill worker. Of Wolfe's arrest, he says, "Scoundrel! Serves him right! After all our kindness that night!" (50).

Until the Quaker arrives at Hugh's deathbed, Deborah alone recognizes his pain. During her last visit to his cell before his death, Deborah finally realizes the depths of his despair:

> She peered closely into his face. Something she saw there made her draw suddenly back,—something . . . that lay beneath the pinched, vacant look it had caught since the trial, or the curious gray shadow that rested on it. That gray shadow,—yes, she knew what that meant. She had often seen it creeping over women's faces for months, who died at last of slow hunger or consumption. That meant death, distant, lingering: but this—Whatever it was the woman saw, or thought she saw, used as she was to crime and misery, seemed to make her sick with a new horror. (53)

However, Deborah, a prisoner herself suffering from the same despair, has no personal or cultural resources to help Hugh. She can only kneel in an adjacent cell with her ear to a crack in the wall hoping to hear something while willing herself not to cry out. Powerless to stop Hugh, she convinces herself that he knows what is best for himself and, since she can imagine no argument that would convince him to accept his condition, she can only support his decision. In her deep affection and sympathy for Hugh, Deborah approximates the caring exhibited by the Quaker woman, but she lacks the capacity and perhaps the courage to transcend the reality of her condition.[11] Only the anonymous Quaker possesses both the kindness and the ability to express that kindness in the form of aid to Hugh.

As the Quaker woman knows, she has arrived too late to save Hugh and can only turn her efforts to rescuing Deborah from a similar fate. Deborah begs her to take Hugh's body and bury it "out where t'air blows," thus saving him from the eternal condemnation of burial in the town yard "under t' mud and ash" that represents the source of his downfall (62). "The Quaker hesitated, but only for a moment," and then, recognizing in Deborah many of the same needs that tormented Hugh, "put her strong arm around Deborah and led her to the window." There she shows Deborah the idyllic site of the Quaker community, where she promises to bury Hugh in a place where the "light lies warm" on the hills and the river "and the winds of God blow all the day" (62).

In its contrast to the smoky town, this harmonious scene recalls the contrast between Rachel Halliday's kitchen and the world of the slave traders. However, for Deborah, unlike for Eliza and George, vision becomes reality. After Deborah serves her three-year prison sentence, "the Quaker began her work." At the end of the story the fruits of her labors emerge. Deborah, "old, deformed . . . her worn face, pure and meek," sits with the Friends in the meetinghouse, "a homely pine house . . . niched into the very place where the light is warmest, the air freest" (63). Having adopted the Quaker life-style, Deborah has become "a woman much loved by these silent, restful people; more silent than they, more humble, more loving," and she serves as abiding testament to the anonymous Quaker's success (63–64).

Through the work of this anonymous Friend, Quakerism has triumphed where even the more mainstream Christianity that motivates Doctor May has failed. Moving the Quaker woman out of the home and into the worst grime of the industrialized world, Davis, like Stowe, undermines the traditional divisions of public and private. This Quaker woman at work in the world brings with her the familial values of mutual interdependence and support and applies them to the larger family of all humankind. Following a spiritual and communal ethic, she is able to bring fresh air and a sense of possibility into the stifling commercial and industrial world of the iron mills. As a comparison of Deborah's life-style before and after her conversion to Quakerism graphically shows, Davis leaves little doubt about which model offers the most promise for societal reform. As in Stowe's novel, the Quaker woman in Davis's text occupies the story's ethical center and controls its reformist vision. What Davis adds to Stowe's vision is her recognition that if the Quaker woman is to help those in need, she must leave the home and work among them.

The connection between a Quaker woman at work and nine-teenth-century reform efforts is again highlighted in Alcott's *Work: A Story of Experience.* In two characters—Mrs. Sterling and the novel's heroine, Christie Devon—Quaker values come together with the image of a woman at work. A precursor of Theodore Dreiser's Carrie and Stephen Crane's Maggie, Christie is a young girl, on her own for the first time, struggling to free herself from financial dependence on an uncle by making her own way in the city. The novel's feminist theme is clear from Christie's opening statement—"Aunt Betsey, there's going to be a new Declaration of Independence" (5)[12]—as well as in her reasons for wishing to be independent:

> I'm old enough to take care of myself; and if I'd been a boy, I should
> have been told to do it long ago. I hate to be dependent; and now
> there's no need of it, I can't bear it any longer. (5)

In a search reminiscent of that of Elizabeth Ashbridge following her period of indenture, Christie experiments with a variety of employment options, including working as a servant, an actress, a governess, and a seamstress. During her quest, she meets three women who profoundly influence her life. While a parlor servant to the wealthy Mrs. Stuart, Christie comes to know Hepsey Johnson, "a tall, gaunt woman, bearing the tragedy of her race written in her face, with its melancholy eye, subdued expression, and the pathetic patience of a wronged dumb animal" (19–20). In this brief period of servitude, Christie experiences a muted version of the indignities and injustices she believes Hepsey must have felt during her earlier life as a slave. Like the slaves, Christie loses control over her own identity when Mrs. Stuart, finding "Christie Devon" too long a name for a servant girl, decides to call her Jane. She also informs her new servant that she must know her place and be as unobtrusive as possible, blending in with the background rather than asserting her individual personality. Having lost her identity, Christie must symbolically forge another. For her, this process begins with a friendship with Hepsey, whose stories fascinate Christie more than the "elegant sameness" of her employer's life:

> [Hepsey's] story was like many another; yet, being the first Christie
> had ever heard, and told with the unconscious eloquence of one

who had suffered and escaped, it made a deep impression on her,
bringing home to her a sense of obligation so forcibly that she
began to pay a little part of the great debt which the white race
owes the black. (26)

This newly acquired sense of obligation to others becomes central to
Christie's developing moral convictions, as she begins a search for a
spiritual home that runs parallel to her search for employment. When
Christie learns that Hepsey works primarily to earn enough money to
allow her to return to the South in order to purchase her mother's
freedom, she finds it strange and disappointing that her wealthy
employer does not feel any obligation to help her in her cause.

Christie is also influenced by a woman who works with her when
she is a seamstress in "a large and well-conducted mantua-making
establishment" (102). Preferring to spend her evenings reading, "for she
had the true New England woman's desire for education, and read or
studied for the love of it" (103), Christie has only a few acquaintances
among the girls she works with, and only one true friend:

> Among the girls was one quiet, skilful creature, whose black dress,
> peculiar face, and silent ways attracted Christie. Her evident desire
> to be let alone amused the new comer at first, and she made no
> effort to know her. But presently she became aware that Rachel
> watched her with covert interest, stealing quick, shy glances at her
> as she sat musing over her work. (103)

Christie, attracted by Rachel's Quaker-like appearance, gradually
brings her out of her shell with the language and techniques of
courtship. She "wooed" her, "patiently and gently as a lover might,"
bringing her flowers, paying her compliments, and eventually changing her seat to be closer to her (104). In using the courtship ritual to
describe their developing relationship, Alcott indicates the depth of
the friendship and the love that these two women come to share.
Christie is consequently surprised and hurt when she learns that
Rachel will lose her job because she is a "fallen woman" and thus an
undesirable influence on the young women in the shop, who, the
owner hopes, are shining examples of true womanhood. Once again
acting on her belief in a communal obligation to help others, Christie,

appalled that Rachel is being fired instead of being helped, asks of the owner, "[W]here will she go if you send her away? . . . What stranger will believe in her if we, who have known her so long, fail to befriend her now?" (108). Christie alone supports her friend, sacrificing her own job in Rachel's defense.

Although she is not yet a member of the Society of Friends, Christie has a sense of morality and duty that corresponds to Quaker values. Her propinquity to the Quakers also stems from her almost instinctive association with precisely those women most unable to participate in the dominant nineteenth-century culture. With this predilection toward Quaker principles, her joy is apparent when, at her new place of domestic service, the door is opened by Mrs. Sterling, "the dearest of little Quaker ladies . . . with such an air of peace and good-will that the veriest ruffian, coming to molest or make afraid, would have found it impossible to mar the tranquillity [*sic*] of that benign old face" (171). Mrs. Sterling welcomes Christie "into a room whose principal furniture seemed to be books, flowers, and sunshine" and then directs her to her bedroom—"a room as plain and white and still as a nun's cell" (171). Donning an apron, Christie goes to work in the kitchen. Like Rachel Halliday's, it is "tidy with the immaculate order of which Shakers and Quakers alone seem to possess the secret,—a fragrant, shining cleanliness, that made even black kettles ornamental and dish-pans objects of interest" (172). The house and the principles it exudes have almost magical powers on Christie, who

> felt as if she had left the troublous world behind her, and shutting
> out want, solitude, and despair, had come into some safe, seclud-
> ed spot full of flowers and sunshine, kind hearts, and charitable
> deeds. (188)

In the Sterling home, Christie discovers that her search is over. Not only has she found enjoyable employment, but she has symbolically moved into the Quaker fold and gained the spiritual and moral context within which to articulate and to deepen her beliefs. The house becomes a place of healing, a "beneficent, unostentatious asylum" offering "salvation" (191) and familial contentment, as "mistress and maid soon felt like mother and daughter, and Christie often said she did not care for any other wages" (189). On a more literal level,

Christie also finds a family within the Sterling home when she agrees to marry Mrs. Sterling's son, David, and adopts the Quaker life-style.

Unlike earlier Quaker heroines like Edith Morrison, whose marriage mutes her call to public duty, Christie's Quakerism, anchored firmly in the principles of equality and independence across gender lines, finds even stronger expression after her marriage. Perhaps owing to Mrs. Sterling's own sense of self-assuredness that allowed her to marry outside the meeting and yet still remain a devout Quaker, the Quakerism Christie ultimately comes to know and practice deviates slightly from traditional Quaker customs. Its unconventionality is reflected in David's decision, after long and tortuous deliberation, to enlist in the army and his mother's ability to honor his choice. Already dressed in his uniform, he kneels before his mother in one evening to tell her:

> The little Quaker cap went down on the broad shoulder, and the only answer he heard was a sob. . . . What happened in the twilight no one ever knew; but David received promotion for bravery in a harder battle than any he was going to, and from his mother's breast a decoration more precious to him than the cross of the Legion of Honor from a royal hand. (283)

Mrs. Sterling's courage in accepting David's enlistment corresponds to Christie's resolve to enlist along with him and work in the hospital: "There was fire in Christie's eyes and a flush on her cheek now, as she stood up with the look of a woman bent on doing well her part" (281).

Christie's wedding signifies her adoption of the Quaker belief in equality and simplicity. Refusing to wear "the pretty silvery silk" dress her friends offer, she chooses instead to be married, as David will be, in uniform. Her hospital uniform, made of "soft, gray, woollen [*sic*] stuff," recalls the simplicity of Quaker drab, visibly linking her independence of spirit to her Quaker convictions (292).

The power of Quakerism to provide a viable alternative cultural model is not hidden in Alcott's novel as it is in much of the earlier fiction. Not only is it one of her major themes throughout the book, but it is a motif that becomes even more overt in the closing chapters. After the war and the death of her husband, Christie yokes her Quaker convictions with activism, assuming a prominent role in the campaign to improve working conditions for women. Nearly twenty years after leaving her uncle's home seeking independence, she becomes a respected public speaker, effective because she understands from firsthand experience the horrors faced by the working women whom she addresses.

The link between her Quaker sense of duty and her public activism is inescapable in the description of her first speech. Sitting in the audience and listening to a series of ineffectual speakers, Christie, like her Quaker foremothers, feels "a sudden and uncontrollable impulse" that makes her "rise in her place and ask leave to speak." Refusing an offer to ascend the dias, she remains on the lowest step, saying, "I am better here, thank you; for I have been and mean to be a working-woman all my life" (332). Then, with the same kind of power described by those who heard eighteenth-century preachers like Ashbridge, Christie speaks "in a clear, steady voice, with the sympathetic undertone to it that is so magical in its effect"; her time on the stage as an actress "stood her in good stead now." Christie is moved by the spirit:

> [W]ords came faster than she could utter them, thoughts pressed upon her, and all the lessons of her life rose vividly before her to give weight to her arguments, value to her counsel, and the force of truth to every sentence she uttered. (332)

No doubt the Quaker meeting would have authorized her speech as genuine and her motivation pure.

In *Work* the covert implications attached to Quaker women characters in earlier novels receive overt acknowledgment. Christie firmly weds the radical dimensions of the Quaker ethic to a form of feminist activism. Alcott shows how the Quaker tradition of equality and independence that empowers Christie's assumption of her rights and responsibility to those around her situates her at precisely the right place to move into leadership roles in reform movements seeking to aid or to protect the rights of others.

7

Epilogue

The character of Christie Devon in Louisa May Alcott's *Work: A Story of Experience* brings the discussion of fictional Quaker women full circle—back to a comparison with one of her eighteenth-century foremothers, Elizabeth Ashbridge. The striking similarities between Christie's story and Ashbridge's raise questions about whether Alcott had perhaps read one of the many versions of Ashbridge's narrative produced throughout the nineteenth century. This speculation is fueled by Bronson Alcott's (Louisa's father) well-documented contacts with numerous Quakers he met through his friend, abolitionist William Lloyd Garrison. Owing in part to these contacts, Bronson came to value personal and direct experiences of God, despite the suspicion with which even the most liberal Protestant denominations of his day continued to view Quaker tenets. From one Friend he encountered in his early travels, he received copies of John Woolman's *Journal* and William Penn's *No Cross, No Crown* (Saxton 24, 58, 67). His possession of these books, his sustained contact with Quakers, his wife's close ties to Quaker feminist Lucretia Mott, and his sympathy with Friends' general beliefs all demonstrate an unusually strong interest in Quakerism within the Alcott home—an interest that could plausibly have afforded his daughter access to so popular a narrative as Ashbridge's.

While the nineteenth-century world of Alcott's novel differs greatly from Ashbridge's eighteenth-century world, the movements of Christie and Ashbridge through their respective cultures are both governed by the motif of the search. Each of them tries her hand at a variety of jobs so as to find a place in society, independent of parental support and influence. Even the catalogs of the jobs they hold or contemplate are similar. They both work in domestic service, one as a hired girl and one as an indentured servant; both are actresses; both earn money through needlework; and both work with children, one as a governess, and the other as a teacher. Paralleling their search for employment is the more important search for a spiritual foundation, a search that ends for both of them within the Quaker tradition. Furthermore, for each of them, Quaker teachings combine with stage experience to empower them to speak forcefully in public arenas—Ashbridge as a preacher, and Christie as a leader of a feminist reform movement.

Any comparison between a fictional character and an historical figure has obvious limitations, but the similarities between Christie and Ashbridge are instructive here because Christie's character development pointedly traces the principles Ashbridge espoused and demonstrated in her own life a century earlier. Ashbridge and the Quaker women of her generation had to struggle to understand their experience as a continuation of the tradition of seventeenth-century Quaker martyrdom. They also had to find ways to maintain their identity of opposition in an era without visible martyrs. For Ashbridge, this necessitated a self-definition linking her personal trials with the corporate history of Quakerism. In forming this identity, she absorbed from the early martyrs the courage necessary to endure and to overcome the abuses heaped upon her.

However, even as she gained personal power, Ashbridge found her sense of Quaker duty—the same sense of duty that had led others to martyrdom a century earlier—compelling her to assume an active role within the meeting by expressing her convictions and becoming a preacher. Building on the sense of duty that compelled Ashbridge and others to become preachers, nineteenth-century women found their sense of duty carrying them logically into leadership roles in numerous reform movements. Fueled by the tradition of female empowerment within the meeting, Ashbridge spoke powerfully for Quaker causes within the Quaker community, and her nineteenth-century descendants—literary and historical—were able to move smoothly and naturally to the forefront of broader public reform movements. The act of coming to language—the site of struggle, abuse, and dislocation for

Ashbridge—becomes an ordeal that is almost taken for granted by later Quaker women. It sets nineteenth-century women apart from their contemporaries who, lacking the Quaker tradition, were less prepared to assume public roles. The heritage of equality behind Quaker women's assumption of authority carried particular weight in the emergent democratic society permeated by the rhetoric of egalitarianism, making their reformist positions particularly attractive to many non-Quakers. Like Ashbridge, these Quaker women learned to find much strength in their power to influence the attitudes and actions of the non-Quaker world, whose support and aid they often won for their reform agendas.

The figure of the Quaker woman throughout nineteenth-century fiction suggests that her ability to influence and affect those around her was a highly potent and subversive force, especially among women. Taken to its extreme, the Quaker ethic posits a communitarian cooperative society, shared equally by men and women, that radically challenged dominant individualistic ideology. Different nineteenth-century authors envisioned varying degrees of success for this new cultural order, but almost all saw the potential or the danger within it for radical cultural critique and change.

Elizabeth Ashbridge obviously could not have foreseen the broader historical context of her actions. Nonetheless, as she found a way to empower herself, she and her contemporaries also provided a model of empowerment useful for the authors who wrote the Quaker woman into nineteenth-century fiction. Perhaps, in light of her muted triumph in knowing that she had brought Mr. Sullivan, her greatest adversary, to recognize the validity of Quaker principles, she would have believed, with her fictional successors, in the possibility of reforming American culture by putting into practice the Quaker belief in equality. Given her own "Remarkable Experiences," Ashbridge might finally have been able to recognize her own peculiar power in effecting that reformation.

Notes

1

Introduction

1. "Remarkable Experiences of Elizabeth Ashbridge" is the title given to this narrative by Edmund Hatcher, an early twentieth-century editor of her manuscript. In so naming the text, Hatcher employs a phrase often found in the stock openings of Quaker spiritual autobiographies.

2. The extreme popularity of *Pamela; or, Virtue Rewarded* would almost guarantee Ashbridge's acquaintance with the novel. An immediate best-seller upon its publication in 1740, the novel spawned a widespread "Pamela" craze, with likenesses of the title character appearing on everything from china cups to ladies' fans. In addition, numerous parodies of the novel were published, including Fielding's *Shamela* (1741) and *Joseph Andrews* (1742).

2

"Better Be Hanged"

1. All references to Elizabeth Ashbridge's narrative are to Daniel B. Shea's edition, published in *Journeys in New Worlds: Early American Women's Narratives,* William Andrews, gen. ed. (Madison: University of Wisconsin Press, 1990) 147–80. This edition is based on two early manuscript versions of Ashbridge's narrative, both in the Bevan-Naish Library of the Woodbrooke Quaker Study Centre in Birmingham, England.

2. Estimates of the early Quaker population's size vary considerably among historians. Rufus Jones's 1911 estimates provide a relative sense of their numbers and their geographic distribution in 1700. At this time, Quakers were the largest population in

North Carolina, on Rhode Island's south shore, and on Long Island; they formed half the population of Newport, one-third the population in Maine and New Hampshire, and were an "influential body" in New York; 25,000 Quakers lived in Pennsylvania, 6,000 in New Jersey, 4,000 to 5,000 in Virginia, 4,000 to 5,000 in the Carolinas, 3,000 in Maryland, and 3,000 in southern Massachusetts (xv–xvi).

3. In *The Quaker Home,* a 1891 novel by George Fox Tucker, the comments of a non-Quaker child to his Quaker friend typifies this attitude: "You must lead a dreadfully stupid life. Why aren't Quakers like other people? What's the good of leading such dull and quiet lives?" (17).

4. For a list of the published attacks on Quakers, see Joseph Smith's *Bibliotheca Anti-Quakeriana*. Although not exhaustive, Smith's work lists hundreds of references to writings attacking Quakers and to Quaker responses to their attackers.

5. On 7 August 1656, two days after Mary Austin and Anne Fisher were shipped out of Massachusetts, eight more Quakers arrived: Christopher Holder, John Copeland, Thomas Thurston, Willima Brend, Mary Prince, Sarah Gibbons, Mary Whetherhead, and Dorothy Waugh (Jones 36).

6. The petition to King Charles II included the following partial list of offenses:

> "Two Honest and Innocent Women stripped stark naked and searched after such an inhumane manner, as modesty will not permit particularly to mention.
>
> "Twelve strangers in that Country, but freeborn of this Nation, received twenty-three Whippings, the most of them being with a Whip of three Cords, with knots at the ends, and laid on with as much strength as they could be by the Arm of their Executioner, the stripes amounting to Three hundred and seventy.
>
> "Sixty-four Imprisonments of the Lord's People, for their obedience to his Will, amounting to five hundred and nineteen weeks, much of it being very cold weather, and the Inhabitants kept in Prison in harvest time, which was very much to their losse....
>
> "Fines laid upon the Inhabitants for meeting together and edifying one another, as the Saints ever did; and for refusing to Swear, it being contrary to Christ's Command, amounting to about a thousand pound...; many Families, in which there are many Children, are almost ruined, by these unmerciful proceedings.
>
> "Five kept Fifteen dayes (in all) without food, and Fifty eight dayes shut up close by the Jaylor, and had none that he knew of; and from some of them he stopt up the windows hindering them from convenient air.
>
> "One laid Neck and Heels in Irons for fifteen hours.
>
> "One very deeply burnt in the right hand with the letter H after he had been whipt with above Thirty stripes.
>
> "One chained the most part of Twenty dayes to a Logg of wood in an open Prison in the Winter-time.

"Three had their right Ears cut off by the Hangman in the Prison. . . .

"At a General Court in Boston, they made an Order that those who had not inherewithal made answer to the fines that were laid upon them (for their Consciences) should be sold as Bond-men, and Bond-women to Barbados, Virginia, or any of the English Plantations. (Burrough, 17–19)

7. Strangers in many early seventeenth-century communities in British North America, viewed as potential sources of social and political difficulties, were often "warned out" by community officials. This practice reflected the English theory of inhabitance that regarded each town as a corporation with the right to exclude anyone not a part of that corporation. For a discussion of the practice of turning away people who might need public aid, see Trattner, *From Poor Law to Welfare State*, 18ff.

8. In "Singing in the Spirit in Early Quakerism," Kenneth L. Carroll documents the existence of this group of radical Quakers. He provides several accounts of Quakers who, moved to song while imprisoned, converted their jailers through their music. In addition, he finds references to a preaching tradition that existed among English and Irish Quakers prior to 1675—perhaps the tradition to which Roger Williams refers—where the women preachers chanted their sermons.

9. For a discussion of the seventeenth-century Quaker practice of "going naked as a sign" and the historical precedents for this practice, see Kenneth L. Carroll, "Early Quakers and 'Going Naked as a Sign.'"

10. This argument for scriptural precedent for women preachers remained strong throughout the nineteenth century. For example, Jarena Lee, the first female preacher in the African Methodist Episcopal church, used the same twofold argument almost 200 years later to justify her right to preach. The publishers of her 1836 narrative suggest that her editor may have been a Quaker. See Jarena Lee, *The Life and Religious Experiences of Jarena Lee.*

11. For the history of Van Heemskerck's *Quaker Meeting* and a collection of the engravings that it inspired, see William I. Hull, "Egbert van Heemskerk's 'Quaker Meeting.'"

12. Several sermons in Joseph Smith's *A Descriptive Catalogue of Friends' Books* are labeled "tub lectures." In *A Glimpse of Sion's Glory,* Philip Gura links the practice with the Baptist tradition, though the iconography in that tradition suggests that the practice may refer to preachers standing in a tub, rather than on one (39, 99). The practice of preaching from a tub is also alluded to in Virginia Woolf's novel *Mrs. Dalloway*: "At Hyde Park Corner on a tub she stands preaching . . ." (New York: Harcourt, Brace and World, 1952), 151. The tub also calls to mind the phrase "tub-thumping." *Brewer's Dictionary of Phrase and Fable,* comp. Rev. E. Cobham Brewer (Philadelphia: J. B. Lippincott, 1931), defines "tub-thumper" as "a blustering, ranting, public speaker; a 'stump-orator.' In allusion to the tub frequently used as a rostrum at open-air meetings" (1097).

13. John Greenleaf Whittier refers to Heemskerck's painting in his 1872 poem, "Pennsylvania Pilgrim" (103–12):

> One faith alone, so broad that all mankind
> Within themselves its secret witness find,—
> Scholar and peasant, lord and serf, allied,
> The polished Penn and Cromwell's Ironside.
> As still in Hemskerck's Quaker Meeting, face
> By face in Flemish detail, we may trace
> How loose-mouthed boor and fine ancestral grace
> Sat in close contrast,—the clipt-headed churl,
> Broad market-dame, and simple serving-girl
> By skirt of silk and periwig in curl! (107)

Whittier appended a note to the poem that emphasizes Heemskerck's artistic reputation:

> The Quakers' Meeting,—a painting by E. Hemskerck (supposed to be Egbert Hemskerck the younger, son of Egbert Hemskerk the older), in which William Penn and others—among them Charles II, or the Duke of York—are represented along with the rudest and most stolid class of the British rural population at that period. Hemskerck came to London from Holland with King William in 1689. He delighted in wild, grotesque subjects, such as the nocturnal intercourse of witches and the temptation of St. Anthony. Whatever was strange and uncommon attracted his free pencil. Judging from the portrait of Penn, he must have drawn his faces, figures and costumes from life, although there may be something of caricature in the convulsed attitudes of two or three of the figures. (Whittier 521)

14. In *Wayward Puritans,* Kai Erickson suggests another connection between Hutchinson, the early Quaker movement in Massachusetts, and the Salem witchcraft craze of 1692. Both Hutchinson's antinomian beliefs and Quakerism are similar to orthodox Puritan theology, yet both are defined by the Puritans as deviant. Erickson argues that in their extreme concern for maintaining orthodoxy in Massachusetts and in their definition of people like Hutchinson and the early Quakers as deviants and as threats to their system, Puritans were in fact *creating* deviancy in their community, thereby seeking to define more clearly the boundaries of the orthodox and thus strengthen their community. Communal fears and deviancy go hand in hand in Erickson's theory. He argues that the more a community fears the deviant, the more likely the members of that community will be to find deviance all around them.

15. Amy Schrager Lang's *Prophetic Woman* provides a definitive discussion of Anne Hutchinson as the progenitor of a tradition of female dissent in New England literature, and demonstrates how Hutchinson's story has been altered throughout the seventeenth, eighteenth, and nineteenth centuries to fulfill the distinct cultural needs of each of these periods.

16. Rosemary Skinner Keller discusses several lesser-known women dissenters in

New England in "New England Women: Ideology and Experience in First Generation Puritanism (1630–1650)" (Ruether and Keller 139–43, and passim).

17. All references to Hawthorne's "The Gentle Boy" are to the Centenary Edition
of the Works of Nathaniel Hawthorne, *Twice-Told Tales* (Columbus: Ohio State University Press, 1974), 9:68–105.

3

Power and Prestige as a Public Friend

1. While Quakers continued to possess considerable political and economic power
in Pennsylvania in the 1750s, their population was decreasing. James Logan, onetime
secretary to William Penn and prominent Philadelphia Quaker, estimated that as early
as 1702 fewer than one-third of all Philadelphians were Quakers. Frederick Tolles
argues that Logan's estimate is low but agrees that Quakers were no longer dominant
in Philadelphia at the beginning of the eighteenth century. According to Tolles, there
were 800 Quaker families in Philadelphia by 1750, constituting slightly more than one-
fourth of the city's population (*Meeting House* 231–32).

2. Tolles suggests that the Quakers were not absorbed in the bursts of evangelical
enthusiasm of the Great Awakening because of their ongoing efforts at differentiating
and separating themselves from the dominant religious cultures in Pennsylvania. By
the time Whitefield and the other itinerant preachers reached the middle colonies, the
majority of Quakers were "so thoroughly insulated from contact with other religious
bodies that the waves of religious enthusiasm that boiled all about them scarcely
touched the hems of their garments" (*Meeting House* 233–34). The Quakers' isolation,
Tolles argues, is evidence of a shift from their religious enthusiasm in the seventeenth
century to their quietism in the eighteenth. They thus moved from an essentially
prophetic mode to a more mystical mode of worship (*Quakers* 91ff).

3. Numerous Quaker writers comment on the skill and effectiveness of Whitefield's preaching, evidence that although most Quakers were not among his converts,
many heard him preach. James Logan wrote that "none can be long a stranger to
George Whitefield," who "by good language, a better utterance, and engaging manner,
and a powerful voice . . . gained much at first on most sorts of people" (Tolles, *Quakers*
100). Most Quakers, however, coupled their admiration of Whitefield's abilities with
disapproval of the doctrine of predestination that he preached. Richard Hockley of
Philadelphia judged "that shining light the Reverend Mr. Whitefield" to be "a very
sincere person, zealous for his Master's cause, and justly admired for his elegant
though plain language." While he praised Whitefield for "endeavoring to reclaim a
wicked, vicious, and sinful age," he hastened to add that:

I am steadfast to the Quakers' principles which I have always professed, and
like[d] Mr. Whitefield when he preached them up until he derogated from

them and got into the scheme of reprobation which by no means squares
with the notions that I hold after a mature and deliberate consideration of
the means of salvation through Christ. (Tolles, *Quakers* 98–99)

The frenzy surrounding Whitefield's visits, however, concerned Quaker Judah Foulke,
who wrote to the Burlington Meeting that Philadelphia was

in an uproar about this Whitefield. For my part I once had a good opinion
of the man, but I am afraid he has let his zeal carry him too far in some
things, in pulling down the writings of them who are dead and not here to
vindicate their own cause, which seems to have too much self and bigotry, to
pull down other[s] and set up himself. (Tolles, *Quakers* 99)

Despite the plethora of negative Quaker response to Whitefield and his fellow itinerants, some Quakers fell under their spell and renounced their Quaker teachings in
favor of the doctrine of predestination. In the 11 June 1741 *Pennsylvania Gazette,* editor
Benjamin Franklin printed news of Gilbert Tennent's baptizing eight former Quakers,
one of whom had been a minister in the Society of Friends (Tolles, *Quakers* 99).
Moreover, in his autobiography, Franklin amusingly relates the story of "Friend Hop-
kinson," who was so moved by Whitefield's preaching that he attempted to borrow
money for a donation (134).

These reactions are not as surprising as they might at first seem. With their
emphasis on inward reflection and on an indwelling of the Holy Spirit, the Awakeners
shared with the Quakers a temperament even the staunchest of Friends could respect.
Up to the point of Whitefield's emphasis on predestination, the differences between
the itinerants of the Great Awakening and the Quakers were more stylistic than
substantive.

Opponents of the Awakening, who considered its excesses a dangerous form of
mass emotionalism, seized this affinity between the Quaker temperament and that of
the evangelists as a weapon with which to beat down the revival. To be "Quakerish"
was to be dangerous, and Charles Chauncy, the revival's greatest opponent, hurled the
"Quakerish" accusation at Whitefield. For Chauncy in the 1740s, the evangelists had
fallen into "enthusiasm," a mental disorder leading inevitably to a sad end. Chauncy
recognized its manifestations: they reminded him of his boyhood encounters with
Quakers, when he was

an eye witness to such violent agitations and foamings, in a boisterous
female speaker, as [he] could not behold but with surprise and wonder.
(Heimert and Miller 232)

From the Quaker perspective, however, the Awakeners were "Quakerish" only up to a
point. Then dangerous doctrine intervened, and the Friends opted to remain steadfast

to their own Inner Light. In "The Preacher," a poem about Whitefield's career, the nineteenth-century poet John Greenleaf Whittier nicely captures the Quaker's ability to withstand the heat of enthusiasm (Whittier 69–74):

> With zeal wing-clipped and white-heat cool,
> Moved by the spirit in grooves of rule,
> No longer harried, and cropped, and fleeced,
> Flogged by sheriff and cursed by priest,
> But by wiser counsels left at ease
> To settle quietly on his lees,
> And, self-concentred, to count as done
> The work which his fathers well begun,
> In silent protest of letting alone,
> The Quaker kept the way of his own,
> A non-conductor among the wires,
> With coat of asbestos proof to fires. (72–73)

As Whittier suggests, the Quakers' past bore great similarity to the realities of the revivalist temperament, and this is perhaps one reason that so many Quakers felt compelled to describe their reactions to the Great Awakening.

4. Richard Bauman provides a thorough discussion of the ambiguity in Quaker attitudes toward speaking and maintaining silence. See "Speaking in the Light," 144–60.

5. The letter, bearing fifty-seven signatures of prominent Quakers from Pennsylvania and New Jersey, dated "the 16th day of the 3rd month 1752," is in the archives of the Library of the Religious Society of Friends, Friends' House, London. William Hammons, a Friend mentioned in Ashbridge's narrative (206), is also among the signers.

6. Aaron Ashbridge to Israel Pemberton, 11 February 1757, Quaker Collection, Haverford College Library, Haverford, Conn.

7. The relative happiness of Elizabeth and Aaron Ashbridge's marriage is difficult to judge. Aaron's lamentation written upon receiving news of Elizabeth's death gives some sense of the depth of his feeling for her (see E. Ashbridge 171–72). However, as J. William Frost reports, letters between Quaker couples habitually emphasized harmony, and there were few quarrels within these marriages deemed severe enough to bring before the meeting (181–82).

8. Tolles estimates that between 1650 and 1700, nearly 150 Quaker men and women from Great Britain visited the meetings in colonial America. This "incessant traveling back and forth across the Atlantic" continued without waning throughout much of the eighteenth century (*Quakers* 13–14). The extensiveness of that travel is documented by one minister, Samuel Fothergill, who records an itinerary for one twenty-month trip covering 8,765 miles (Janney 325).

4

Narrating a Life of "Uncommon Occurrences"

1. Catherine Phillips, for example, begins her narrative with the following: "As the dealings of the Almighty with me from my youth have been singular, and are worthy to be retained in remembrance with thankfulness, I have committed to writing some remarkable circumstances of my life" (3).

2. Jane Hoskens writes of "the tender dealings of a merciful God, in visiting my soul" (3), and Catherine Phillips credits the "dealings of the Almighty from [her] youth" (3).

3. In her study of eighteenth-century British autobiographies and novels, Patricia Meyer Spacks views spiritual autobiography as one of two forms of self-expression available to women:

> Spiritual autobiography provided a respectable mode of expression for the regenerate female; actresses and women of dubious repute published their life stories as part of their more or less scandalous self display. Throughout the eighteenth century women of reputation almost never offered for publication accounts of their lives except with heavy overlays of piety.

Spacks also contends that strong similarities exist between the construction of the self in letters and diaries of reputable women and the "sensationalized stories of female adventurers" (*Imagining* 72). For a discussion of the scandalous stories, see Felicity Nussbaum, "Heteroclites: The Gender of Character in the Scandalous Memoirs," passim.

4. Eakin provides a thorough discussion of the fictional nature of the autobiographical self, as well as a survey of the relevant scholarship, in *Fictions in Autobiography* (passim). For an overview of current studies of the creation of self in women's personal narratives, see Sidonie Smith, *A Poetics of Women's Autobiography*, passim.

5. Janet Gunn formulates her theory of autobiography as a culture-based form in response to "classical" theories of the genre, which argue that the "true self" is timeless and unchanging and that access to the self requires a separation of the self from the world in which it exists (7–8). She also rejects both what she calls the "antimetaphysical" view, which argues that the self does not exist outside of language, and the deconstructionist view of the self as "a failed version of the autobiographer's real self, which is presumed buried under its various and changing appearances" (30). Each of these perspectives fails to account for what Gunn calls "the human, and even religious" significance of autobiography (31).

6. For a discussion of the Puritan morphology of conversion and the role of the conversion narrative in the Puritan congregation, see Edmund S. Morgan, *Visible Saints*, 87–93.

7. From Ashbridge's narrative perspective as a Quaker minister, her elopement would have been particularly problematic. The 1743 Philadelphia Meeting voiced special concern for "young Friends [who] keep company for marriage with non-Friends or marry without parental consent" (Frost 56).

8. Ashbridge's emphasis on alienation from the family distinguishes her text from other eighteenth-century Quaker narratives. While she writes of being cut off from family, her contemporaries stress the supportive families who helped start them on the path that lead to Quakerism. Catherine Phillips, for example, includes in her narrative a lengthy testimony to her parents "who not only professed the truth but had it in possession" (3). John Woolman's journal contains numerous references to his early acquaintance with "the operations of Divine love" owing to the "pious instructions" and care of his parents (23, and passim).

9. The prevalence of sleeping in meetings is attested to by the mention of this practice in the list of "queries" issued by the Philadelphia Meeting in 1743 to help Friends judge the quality of their religious devotion (Frost 56).

10. Seventeenth-century English folklore abounds with references to "spirits," people who coaxed unsuspecting people, often children, onto ships and then sold them to shipmasters as servants (Salinger 9).

11. In a study of indentured servants in Pennsylvania in the eighteenth century, Sharon Salinger finds the most common form of indentureship to be between a servant forced to leave his or her family in search of work and a master who agrees to pay for passage on the ship (10). Often the shipmaster would agree to provide free passage in exchange for the person's signature on indentureship papers, giving him the right to sell that person to a new master once the ship reached the colonies. It was possible, however, for someone to pay for his or her own passage, as Ashbridge claims to have done, without legally being required to enter into bondage. Paying passengers on the ship generally had access to the entire ship, while indentured servants were required to stay below deck (88). Since Ashbridge seems to have had the freedom to roam about the ship, we can presume that at least for much of the trip she was treated as a paying passenger.

12. If the "difference" to which Ashbridge refers involved her master's sexual advances, she had practical as well as moral reasons for concern. Female servants had little protection from such advances, and if they became pregnant they could be punished by having their indentureship contract extended (Frey and Morton 51). For a discussion of punishment of indentured servants, see Semmes 80–118.

13. Ashbridge's emphasis on her own actions runs counter to the pattern of emphasizing passivity that Patricia Meyer Spacks finds in eighteenth-century women's narratives. In these texts she notes

> a tendency to stress what has been done to the protagonist more intensely than what she herself has done—even when she has done a great deal. The fact that the enlargements of self-deprecating fantasy assume this form in women means not simply that the female of the species has traditionally been victimized; it indicates that she makes a mythology of her victimization, verbally converting it into the badge of her freedom. (*Imagining* 73)

14. The connection between God and a lover is not unique to Ashbridge. In *Ornaments for the Daughters of Zion* (1692), Cotton Mather used this same analogy in

delineating the place of widows in seventeenth-century society. He believed that a widow should consider herself "now more than ever belonging to the family of God," and that it should be her "main study and solace to have an interest in that promise, Isai 54.5 THY MAKER IS THY HUSBAND" (Frey and Morton 31).

15. In the last quarter of the seventeenth century, Rhode Island, New Jersey, and Pennsylvania had significant Quaker forces in government (Tolles, *Quakers* 49). But their numbers diminished quickly. By 1700 the Quakers were in the minority in Philadelphia; by 1730 they were a minority throughout Pennsylvania; and after 1756 the Pennsylvania Assembly never had a Quaker majority (Frost 2–3). Much of their loss of political power was voluntary, as Friends realized during the French and Indian War that they could not continue to serve in the assembly without compromising their beliefs (Bacon 72).

5

Gender, Genre, and Cultural Positions

1. As early as 1900 literary critics set Jonathan Edwards and Benjamin Franklin against each other as representatives of a sacred/secular duality in eighteenth-century American culture. See, for example, Barrett Wendell, *A Literary History of America* (New York: Scribner's, 1900), 102–3.

2. All page reference to Woolman's journal are to *The Journal and Major Essays of John Woolman*, ed. Phillips P. Moulton (Richmond, Ind.: Friends United Press, 1989).

3. Israel Pemberton (1715–1779) was part of a prominent Quaker family that assumed religious leadership roles within the meeting and civic leadership throughout colonial Philadelphia. His importance in the literary world of early Quakers is perhaps most evident in the fact that he and his two brothers served on the original editorial committee for John Woolman's *Journal* (Woolman 310).

4. Elizabeth Ashbridge indicates that while still married to Sullivan, she worked as a schoolmaster in Pennsylvania (160) and later in New Jersey (162). Aaron Ashbridge adds that after Sullivan's death, Elizabeth "settled to School keeping, whereby with her Needle she maintained her Self handsomely & by Degrees paid off near all the said Debts in the time of her Widowhood, in which time she also traveled considerably in the Service of Truth" (171).

5. Frederick B. Tolles offers as proof of Quakers' business success the 1769 Philadelphia tax list. Although Quakers constituted only one-seventh of Philadelphia's population at the time, they accounted for over half of those paying taxes over £100. Of the seventeen wealthiest men on the list, eight were Quakers, four had been raised by Quakers, and one had inherited his fortune from his Quaker grandfather (*Quakers* 58).

6. The tension between piousness and worldly success is dramatized in Herman Melville's *Moby Dick* [1851] (New York: Modern Library, 1950). Captain Bildad's appearance marked him as a Quaker:

His own person was the exact embodiment of his utilitarian character. On his long, gaunt body, he carried no spare flesh, no superfluous beard, his chin having a soft, economical nap to it, like the worn nap of his broad-brimmed hat. (75)

Yet "for a pious man, especially for a Quaker, he was certainly rather hard-hearted, to say the least" in anything that concerned making a profit (74). Ishmael's less than flattering portrait of him highlights the conflicts within this "well-to-do, retired whaleman":

Though refusing, from conscientious scruples to bear arms against land invaders, yet himself had illimitably invaded the Atlantic and Pacific; and though a sworn foe to human bloodshed, yet had he in his straight-bodied coat, spilled tuns upon tuns of leviathan gore. How now in the contemplative evening of his days, the pious Bildad reconciled these things in the reminiscence, I do not know; but it did not seem to concern him much, and very probably he had long since come to the sage and sensible conclusion that a man's religion is one thing, and this practical world quite another. This world pays dividends. Rising from a little cabin-boy in short clothes of the drabbest drab, to a harpooner in a broad shad-bellied waistcoat; from that becoming boat-header, chief-mate, and captain, and finally a ship-owner; Bildad . . . had concluded his adventurous career by wholly retiring from active life at the goodly age of sixty, and dedicating his remaining days to the quiet receiving of his well-earned income. (74)

7. According to the *Oxford English Dictionary*, "wet Quaker" was used colloquially as early as 1700 to refer to a Quaker "not very strict in the observance of his sect." It was also used in a more restricted sense to mean "a drunkard of that Sect."

8. In his study of Quaker reform, Jack Marietta finds a "conspicuous absence" of offenses against plain dress or plain speech that came before the meeting (22). Numerous Quaker writers, however, document concern that one's appearance be sufficiently plain. Sarah Stephenson's description of Ashbridge's visit also demonstrates the role of Public Friends in enforcing this testimony.

9. The peculiarity of men who declined to wear wigs is attested to in another eighteenth-century personal narrative, *The Diary of Samuel Sewall*. In Sewall's well-known account of his courtship of Madame Winthrop, he makes particular mention of her desire for him to wear a wig. His refusal to do so marked him as oddity within the society with which Winthrop wished to be associated (963–64).

10. Although Ashbridge also "maintained her Self handsomely" through needle-work (171), she makes no mention of any concern that her needlework be of the plain style.

11. Clothing regulations were strict, but, contrary to the stereotype, eighteenth-century Quakers were not drab. Their clothing was often colorful, though not gaudy. For example, a portrait of three women of the prominent Philadelphia Norris family

shows one gown of blue and crimson, one of deep blue, and one of dark crimson (Tolles, *Meeting House* 126). Even the Quaker apron satirically alluded to in anti-Quaker broadsides and pamphlets was most commonly green or blue (Gummere 133).

12. This arrangement distinguished the American meetinghouses from those in England, where the women's meeting typically met in a small loft or in a detached shed (Bacon 46–47).

6

Elizabeth Ashbridge's Literary Daughters

1. In *Mothers of Feminism*, Margaret Hope Bacon provides statistical evidence of the prominence of Quakers in nineteenth-century reform movements:

> Quaker women comprised thirty percent of the pioneers in prison reform, forty percent of the women abolitionists, and fifteen percent of suffragists born before 1830. (1)

Of particular interest to the case of Elizabeth Ashbridge is Bacon's mention of Alice Jackson Lewis from Ashbridge's own Chester County, Pennsylvania. In 1806 Lewis spoke in the Philadelphia Women's Meeting urging a meeting-wide boycott of cotton, sugar, and all other products made available through slave labor. Prior to this time, such decisions to boycott were made individually (101).

2. The women present at the tea party that became the planning meeting for the Seneca Falls convention were Lucretia Mott, Elizabeth Cady Stanton, Martha Coffin Wright (Mott's sister), Mary Ann McClintock, and Jane Hunt. Of these five women, Stanton was the only one not a member of the Society of Friends. This mix of Quaker and non-Quaker women was, according to Carol Stoneburner, typical of the style of Quaker leadership in the nineteenth century. She notes that "Quaker women have provided various kinds of leadership in the movement of American women into more public spaces," and that "this leadership is always in interaction with other non-Quaker women leaders" (36).

3. The Quaker man in nineteenth-century novels has been largely ignored, along with the Quaker woman. Characters like Cooper's Judge Temple and Melville's Ahab are exceptional for the quantity of commentary they have received. However, these characters' Quakerism has not been of primary interest to critics, who have studied them primarily for their roles as leading characters in "major" American novels. In the lesser known sentimental novels, the Quaker man is often marked by his pacifism, which brings him into conflict with societal prescriptions about military service.

4. All page references to this novel are to [Rebecca Beach], *The Puritan and the Quaker: A Story of Colonial Times* (New York: G. P. Putnam's Sons, 1879).

5. All page references to this novel are to John Neal, *Rachel Dyer: A North Ameri-*

can Story (Portland, Me.: Shirley and Hyde, 1828; Gainsville, Fla.: Scholars' Facsimiles and Reprints, 1964).

6. All page references to this novel are to Eliza Buckminster Lee, *Naomi; or, Boston Two Hundred Years Ago,* 2nd ed. (Boston: Wm. Crosby and H. P. Nichols, 1848).

7. See Amy Schrager Lang's *Prophetic Woman* for a detailed discussion of the ways in which Naomi's fictional trial recalls explicitly the transcripts from Anne Hutchinson's historical court scene. Lang also points outs the inherent differences between Naomi and Hutchinson. Naomi is a young girl lacking Hutchinson's experience, theological sophistication, and willingness to challenge the ministers (159–60).

8. All page references to this novel are to Harriet Beecher Stowe, *Uncle Tom's Cabin; or, Life among the Lowly,* ed. Ann Douglas (1852; New York: Penguin, 1981).

9. Jane Tompkins sees in this scene a more radical message. In her view, Simeon's preening in front of the mirror is indicative of "the position men will occupy in the millennium" (145–46).

10. All page references to this novella are to Rebecca Harding Davis, *Life in the Iron Mills,* ed. Tillie Olsen (1861; New York: Feminist Press, 1985).

11. Sharon Harris presents a detailed analysis of Deborah's role in *Rebecca Harding Davis and American Realism.* She argues that Davis has created a "three-tiered narrative structure" that is a "recreation of the hierarchical social strata of mid–nineteenth-century America." Deborah occupies the middle tier in this scheme and thus functions in the story as a bridge between the world of the mill and the world of the Quaker woman (28ff).

12. All page references to this novel are to Louisa May Alcott, *Work: A Story of Experience,* ed. Joy S. Kasson (1873; New York: Penguin Books, 1994).

Bibliography

Alcott, Louisa May. *Work: A Story of Experience*. 1873. Ed. Joy Kasson. New York: Penguin Books, 1994.

Ashbridge, Elizabeth. *Some Account of the Fore Part of the Life of Elizabeth Ashbridge*. Ed. Daniel B. Shea. In *Journeys in New Worlds: Early American Women's Narratives*. Madison: University of Wisconsin Press, 1990. 147–80.

Ashbridge, Wellington T. *The Ashbridge Book*. Toronto: Copp, Clark Company, 1912.

Axelrod, Alan, ed. *The Colonial Revival in America*. New York: W. W. Norton and Company, 1985.

Bacon, Margaret Hope. *Mothers of Feminism: The Story of Quaker Women in America*. San Francisco: Harper and Row, 1986.

Baltzell, E. Digby. *Puritan Boston and Quaker Philadelphia: Two Protestant Ethics and the Spirit of Class Authority and Leadership*. Boston: Beacon Press, 1979.

Bauman, Richard. "Aspects of Seventeenth-Century Quaker Rhetoric." *Quarterly Journal of Speech* 56 (1970): 67–74.

———. *Let Your Words Be Few: Symbolism of Speaking and Silence among Seventeenth-Century Quakers*. New York: Cambridge University Press, 1983.

———. "Speaking in the Light: The Role of the Quaker Minister." *Explorations in the Ethnography of Speaking*. Ed. Richard Bauman and Joel Sherzer. New York: Cambridge University Press, 1974. 144–60.

[Beach, Rebecca.] *The Puritan and the Quaker: A Story of Colonial Times*. New York: G. P. Putnam's Sons, 1879.

Bednarowski, Mary Farrell. *American Religion: A Cultural Perspective*. Englewood Cliffs, N.J.: Prentice-Hall, 1984.

Benstock, Shari, ed. *The Private Self: Theory and Practice of Women's Autobiographical Writings*. Chapel Hill: University of North Carolina Press, 1988.

Berkin, Carol Ruth, and Mary Beth Norton, eds. *Women of America: A History*. Boston: Houghton Mifflin, 1979.

Bonomi, Patricia U. *Under the Cope of Heaven: Religion, Society, and Politics in Colonial America*. New York: Oxford University Press, 1986.

Brinton, Howard. *Friends for 300 Years: The History and Beliefs of the Society of Friends since George Fox Started the Quaker Movement*. New York: Harper and Brothers, 1952.

———. *Quaker Journals: Varieties of Religious Experience among Friends*. Wallingford, Penn.: Pendle Hill Publications, 1972.

Brodzki, Bella, and Celeste Schenck, eds. *Life/Lines: Theorizing Women's Autobiography*. Ithaca, N.Y.: Cornell University Press, 1988.

Brown, Elizabeth Potts, and Susan Mosher Stuard, eds. *Witnesses for Change: Quaker Women over Three Centuries*. New Brunswick, N.J.: Rutgers University Press, 1989.

Bruss, Elizabeth W. *Autobiographical Acts: The Changing Situation of a Literary Genre*. Baltimore: Johns Hopkins University Press, 1976.

Burrough, Edward. *A Declaration of the Sad and Great Persecution and Martyrdom of the People of God, Called Quakers, in New England for the Worshipping of God*. London: Robert Wilson, 1660.

Butler, Jon. *Awash in a Sea of Faith: Christianizing the American People*. Cambridge, Mass.: Harvard University Press, 1990.

Carroll, Kenneth L. "Early Quakers and 'Going Naked as a Sign.'" *Quaker History* 67 (Autumn 1978): 69–87.

———. "Singing in the Spirit in Early Quakerism." *Quaker History* 73 (Spring 1984): 1–13.

The Character of a Quaker in His True and Proper Colours; or, The Clownish Hypocrite Anatomized. London: T. Egglesfield, 1671.

Cherry, Charles L. "Enthusiasm and Madness: Anti-Quakerism in the Seventeenth Century." *Quaker History* 74 (Fall 1984): 1–24.

Clebsch, Wiliam A. *American Religious Thought: A History*. Chicago: University of Chicago Press, 1973.

Clemens, Paul G. E., and Lucy Simler. "Rural Labor and the Farm Household in Chester County, Pennsylvania, 1750–1820." *Work and Labor in Early America*. Ed. Stephen Innes. Chapel Hill: University of North Carolina Press, 1988. 106–43.

Chu, Jonathan M. *Neighbors, Friends, or Madmen: The Puritan Adjustment to Quakerism in Seventeenth-Century Massachusetts Bay*. Westport, Conn.: Greenwood Press, 1985.

Cott, Nancy F. *The Bonds of Womanhood: "Woman's Sphere" in New England, 1780–1835*. New Haven, Conn.: Yale University Press, 1971.

Culley, Margo, ed. *American Women's Autobiography: Fea(s)ts of Memory*. Madison: University of Wisconsin Press, 1992.

Davidson, Cathy N. *Revolution and the Word: The Rise of the Novel in America*. New York: Oxford University Press, 1986.

Davies, Alan. "Talking in Silence: Ministry in Quaker Meetings." *Styles of Discourse*. Ed. Nikolas Coupland. London: Croom Helm, 1988. 105–37.

Davis, Rebecca Harding. *Life in the Iron Mills*. 1861. Ed. Tillie Olsen. New York: Feminist Press, 1985.

Delbanco, Andrew. *The Puritan Ordeal.* Cambridge, Mass.: Harvard University Press, 1989.

Derounian, Kathryn Zabelle, ed. *The Journal and Occasional Writings of Sarah Wister.* Rutherford, N.J.: Farleigh Dickinson University Press, 1987.

Drinker, Elizabeth. *The Diary of Elizabeth Drinker.* 3 vols. Ed. Elaine Forman Crane. Boston: Northeastern University Press, 1991.

Dunn, Mary Maples. "Saints and Sisters: Congregational and Quaker Women in the Early Colonial Period." *American Quarterly* 30 (Winter 1978): 582–601.

———. "Women of Light." *Women of America: A History.* Ed. Carol Ruth Berkin and Mary Beth Norton. Boston: Houghton Mifflin, 1979. 114–36.

Eakin, Paul John, ed. *American Autobiography: Retrospect and Prospect.* Madison: University of Wisconsin Press, 1991.

———. *Fictions in Autobiography: Studies in the Art of Self Invention.* Princeton, N.J.: Princeton University Press, 1985.

Edkins, Carol. "Quest for Community: Spiritual Autobigraphies of Eighteenth-Century Quaker and Puritan Women in America." *Women's Autobiography: Essays in Criticism.* Ed. Estelle C. Jelinek. Bloomington: Indiana University Press, 1980. 39–52.

Erickson, Kai T. *Wayward Puritans: A Study in the Sociology of Deviance.* New York: John Wiley and Sons, 1966.

Field, Edward. *The Colonial Tavern: A Glimpse of New England Town Life in the Seventeenth and Eighteenth Centuries.* Providence: Preston and Rounds, 1897.

Fisher, Philip. *Hard Facts: Setting and Form in the American Novel.* New York: Oxford University Press, 1987.

Franklin, Benjamin. *The Autobiography of Benjamin Franklin.* Ed. R. Jackson Wilson. New York: Modern Library, 1981.

Frey, Sylvia R., and Marian J. Morton. *New World, New Roles: A Documentary History of Women in Pre-Industrial America.* New York: Greenwood Press, 1986.

Friedman, Susan Stanford. "Women's Autobiographical Selves: Theory and Practice." *The Private Self: Theory and Practice of Women's Autobiographical Writings.* Ed. Shari Benstock. Chapel Hill: University of North Carolina Press, 1988. 34–62.

Frost, J. William. *The Quaker Family in Colonial America: A Portrait of the Society of Friends.* New York: St. Martin's Press, 1973.

Futhey, J. Smith, and Gilbert Cope. *History of Chester County, Pennsylvania, with Genealogical and Biographical Sketches.* Philadelphia: Louis E. Everts, 1881. Facsimile reprint edition, Chester County Historical Society, 1986.

Galenson, David W. *White Servitude in Colonial America: An Economic Analysis.* Cambridge, England: Cambridge University Press, 1981.

Gilpin, John. *The Quakers Shaken; or, A Fire-brand Snatch'd out of the Fire . . .* London, 1653.

Goodbody, Olive C. *Guide to Irish Quaker Records, 1654–1860.* Dublin: Stationery Office for the Irish Manuscripts Commission, 1967.

Greenberg, Douglas. *Crime and Law Enforcement in the Colony of New York, 1691–1776.* Ithaca, N.Y.: Cornell University Press, 1974.

Griffin, Edward M. *Old Brick: Charles Chauncy of Boston, 1705–1787.* Minneapolis: University of Minnesota Press, 1980.

Grimes, Mary Cochran. "Saving Grace among Puritans and Quakers: A Study of 17th and 18th Century Conversion Experiences." *Quaker History* 72 (Spring 1983): 3–26.

Gummere, Amelia Mott. *The Quaker: A Study in Costume.* Philadelphia: Ferris and Leach, 1901.

Gunn, Janet Varner. *Autobiography: Toward a Poetics of Experience.* Philadelphia: University of Pennsylvania Press, 1982.

Gura, Philip F. *A Glimpse of Sion's Glory: Puritan Radicalism in New England, 1620–1660.* Middletown, Conn.: Wesleyan University Press, 1984.

Hall, David D., ed. *The Antinomian Controversy, 1636–1638: A Documentary History.* 1968. Durham, N.C.: Duke University Press, 1990.

Harpham, Geoffrey Galt. "The Language of Conversion." *The Ascetic Imperative in Culture and Criticism.* Chicago: University of Chicago Press, 1987. 91–106.

Harris, Sharon. *Rebecca Harding Davis and American Realism.* Philadelphia: University of Pennsylvania Press, 1991.

Hawkins, Anne Hunsaker. *Archetypes of Conversion: The Autobiographies of Augustine, Bunyan, and Merton.* Lewisburg, Penn.: Bucknell University Press, 1985.

Hawthorne, Nathaniel. "The Gentle Boy." *Twice Told Tales.* The Centenary Edition of the Works of Nathaniel Hawthorne 9. Columbus: Ohio State University Press, 1974. 68–105.

———. "Mrs. Hutchinson." *Tales, Sketches, and Other Papers.* Boston: Houghton Mifflin, 1850. 217–26.

Heimert, Alan, and Perry Miller, eds. *The Great Awakening: Documents Illustrating the Crisis and Its Consequences.* Indianapolis: Bobbs-Merrill, 1967.

Hoffman, Leonore, and Margo Culley, eds. *Women's Personal Narratives: Essay in Criticism and Pedagogy.* New York: Modern Language Association of America, 1985.

Hoskens, Jane. *The Life and Spiritual Sufferings of that Faithful Servant of Christ, Jane Hoskens.* Philadelphia: William Evitt, 1771.

Hull, William I. "Egbert van Heemskerk's 'Quaker Meeting.'" *Bulletin of Friends' Historical Association* 27 (1938): 16–33.

Janney, Samuel M. *History of the Religious Society of Friends, From Its Rise to the Year 1928.* Vol 3. Philadelphia: T. Ellwood Zell, 1867.

Jelinek, Estelle C. *The Tradition of Women's Autobiography: From Antiquity to the Present.* Boston: Twayne Publishers, 1986.

———, ed. *Women's Autobiography: Essays in Criticism.* Bloomington: Indiana University Press, 1980.

Johnson, Dale A. *Women in English Religion, 1700–1925.* New York: Edwin Mellen Press, 1983.

Jones, Rufus M. *The Quakers in the American Colonies.* London: Macmillan and Company, 1911.

Kelley, Robert. *The Cultural Pattern in American Politics: The First Century.* New York: Alfred A. Knopf, 1979.

Kendall, Joan. "The Development of a Distinctive Form of Quaker Dress." *Costume* 19 (1985): 58–74.

Kendall, Paul Murray. *The Art of Biography.* New York: W. W. Norton and Company, 1965.

Knight, Sarah Kemble. "The Journal of Madam Knight." In *Journeys in New Worlds: Early American Women's Narratives.* Ed. Sargent Bush Jr. Madison: University of Wisconsin Press, 1990. 67–116.

Lang, Amy Schrager. *Prophetic Woman: Anne Hutchinson and the Problem of Dissent in the Literature of New England.* Berkeley: University of California Press, 1987.

Lee, Eliza Buckminster. *Naomi; or, Boston Two Hundred Years Ago,* 2nd ed. Boston: Wm. Crosby and H. P. Nichols, 1848.

Lee, Jarena. *The Life and Religious Experiences of Jarena Lee, A Coloured Lady, giving an Account of her Call to Preach the Gospel.* Philadelphia, 1836.

Lee, Mary Catherine. *A Quaker Girl of Nantucket.* Boston: Houghton Mifflin, 1889.

Lee-Whitman, Leanna. "Silks and Simplicity: A Study of Quaker Dress as Depicted in Portraits, 1718–1855." Diss. University of Pennsylvania, 1987.

Levin, David. *In Defense of Historical Literature: Essays on American History, Autobiography, Drama and Fiction.* New York: Hill and Wang, 1967.

Levy, Barry. *Quakers and the American Family: British Settlement in the Delaware Valley.* New York: Oxford University Press, 1988.

Lloyd, Arnold. *Quaker Social History 1669–1738.* Westport, Conn.: Greenwood Press, 1950.

Lovejoy, David S. *Religious Enthusiasm in the New World: Heresy to Revolution.* Cambridge, Mass.: Harvard University Press, 1985.

Lucas, Margaret. *An Account of the Convincement and Call to the Ministry of Margaret Lucas.* Stanford, N.Y.: Daniel Laurence for Henry and John F. Hull, 1803. Micropublished in *History of Women.* No. 615. New Haven, Conn.: Research Publications, 1975.

Marietta, Jack D. *The Reformation of American Quakerism, 1748–1783.* Philadelphia: University of Pennsylvania Press, 1984.

Markham, Gervase. *The English Housewife.* 1615. Ed. Michael R. Best. Kingston, Ontario: McGill-Queen's University Press, 1986.

Mason, Mary G. "The Other Voice: Autobiographies of Women Writers." *Life/Lines: Theorizing Women's Autobiography.* Ed. Bella Brodzki and Celeste Schenck. Ithaca, N.Y.: Cornell University Press, 1988. 19–44.

Moore, R. Laurence. *Religious Outsiders and the Making of Americans.* New York: Oxford University Press, 1986.

Morgan, Edmund S. *Visible Saints.* 1963. Ithaca, N.Y.: Cornell University Press, 1965.

Myers, Albert Cook, ed. *Hannah Logan's Courtship: A True Narrative, as Related in John Smith's Diary.* Philadelphia: Ferris and Leach, 1904.

Neal, John. *Rachel Dyer: A North American Story.* Portland, Me.: Shirley and Hyde, 1928; Gainesville, Fla.: Scholars' Facsimiles and Reprints, 1964.

Neuburg, Victor. "Chapbooks in America: Reconstructing the Popular Reading of Early America." *Reading in America: Literature and Social History.* Ed. Cathy N. Davidson. Baltimore: Johns Hopkins University Press, 1989. 81–113.

Norton, Humphrey. *New England's Ensigne.* London: G. Calvert, 1659. Sabin microfilm #52756.

Nussbaum, Felicity. "Eighteenth-Century Women's Autobiographical Commonplaces." *The Private Self: Theory and Practice of Women's Autobiographical Writings.* Ed. Shari Benstock. Chapel Hill: University of North Carolina Press, 1988. 147–71.

———. "Heteroclites: The Gender of Character in the Scandalous Memoirs." *The New Eighteenth-Century: Theory, Politics, English Literature.* Ed. Felicity Nussbaum and Laura Brown. New York: Methuen, 1987. 144–67.

Olney, James, ed. *Autobiography: Essays Theoretical and Critical.* Princeton, N.J.: Princeton University Press, 1980.

Pennsylvania Historical Survey. *Inventory of Church Archives, Society of Friends in Pennsylvania.* Philadelphia: Friends' Historical Association, 1941.

Phillips, Catherine. *Memoirs of the Life of Catherine Phillips: To Which Are Added Some of Her Epistles.* Philadelphia: Budd and Bartram for Robert Johnson and Company, 1789. Evans Microcard #34371.

Pomerleau, Cynthia S. "The Emergence of Women's Autobiography in England." *Women's Autobiography: Essays in Criticism.* Ed. Estelle C. Jelinek. Bloomington: Indiana University Press, 1980. 21–38.

Prynne, William. *The Quakers Unmasked, and Clearly detected to be but the Spawn of Romish Frogs, Jesuites, and Franciscan Freers . . .* London, 1655.

Rosenblatt, Paul. *John Woolman.* New York: Twayne Publishers, 1969.

Ruether, Rosemary Radford, and Rosemary Skinner Keller. *The Colonial and Revolutionary Periods.* Vol. 2 of *Women and Religion in America.* San Francisco: Harper and Row, 1983.

Salinger, Sharon V. *"To Serve Well and Faithfully": Labor and Indentured Servants in Pennsylvania, 1682–1800.* Cambridge, England: Cambridge University Press, 1987.

Salmon, Marylynn. "Equality or Submersion? Feme Covert Status in Early Pennsylvania." *Women of America: A History.* Ed. Carol Ruth Berkin and Mary Beth Norton. Boston: Houghton Mifflin, 1979. 93–113.

———. *Women and the Law of Property in Early America.* Chapel Hill: University of North Carolina Press, 1986.

Sasson, Diane. *The Shaker Spiritual Narrative.* Knoxville: University of Tennessee Press, 1983.

Saxton, Martha. *Louisa May: A Modern Biography of Louisa May Alcott.* Boston: Houghton Mifflin, 1977.

Semmes, Raphael. *Crime and Punishment in Early Maryland.* Baltimore: Johns Hopkins University Press, 1938.

Sewall, Samuel. *The Diary of Samuel Sewall, 1674–1729.* 2 vols. Ed. M. Halsey Thomas. New York: Farrar, Straus and Giroux, 1973.

Shea, Daniel B. "Elizabeth Ashbridge and the Voice Within." *Journeys in New Worlds: Early American Narratives.* Madison: University of Wisconsin Press, 1990. 119–46.

———. *Spiritual Autobiography in Early America.* 1968. Madison: University of Wisconsin Press, 1988.

Shi, David E. *The Simple Life: Plain Living and High Thinking in American Culture.* New York: Oxford University Press, 1985.

Silverman, Kenneth. *The Life and Times of Cotton Mather.* 1984. New York: Columbia University Press, 1985.

Smith, Abbot Emerson. *Colonists in Bondage: White Servitude and Convict Labor in America, 1607–1776.* Chapel Hill: University of North Carolina Press, 1947.

Smith, Joseph. *Bibliotheca Anti-Quakeriana.* London: Joseph Smith, 1873.

———. *A Descriptive Catalogue of Friends' Books, or Books Written by Members of the Society of Friends, Commonly Called Quakers.* London: Joseph Smith, 1867.

Smith, Sidonie. *A Poetics of Women's Autobiography: Marginality and the Fictions of Self-Representation.* Bloomington: Indiana University Press, 1987.

Smith, Sidonie, and Julia Watson, eds. *De/Colonizing the Subject: The Politics of Gender in Women's Autobiography.* Minneapolis: University of Minnesota Press, 1992.

Spacks, Patricia Meyer. *Imagining a Self: Autobiography and Novel in Eighteenth-Century England.* Cambridge, Mass.: Harvard University Press, 1976.

———. "Selves in Hiding." *Women's Autobiography: Essays in Criticism.* Ed. Estelle C. Jelinek. Bloomington: Indiana University Press, 1980. 112–32.

Speizman, Milton D., and Jane C. Kronick, eds. "A Seventeenth-Century Quaker Women's Declaration." *Signs: Journal of Women in Culture and Society* 1 (Autumn 1975): 231–45.

Stephenson, Sarah. *Memoirs of the Life and Travels, in the Service of the Gospel, of Sarah Stephenson.* Ed. Joseph Gurney Bevan. Philadelphia: Kimber, Conrad, 1807. Micropublished in *History of Women.* No. 625. New Haven, Conn.: Research Publications, 1975.

Stilgoe, John R. *Common Landscape of America, 1580–1845.* New Haven, Conn.: Yale University Press, 1982.

Stoneburner, Carol, and John Stoneburner, eds. *The Influence of Quaker Women on American History.* Lewiston, N.Y.: Edwin Mellen Press, 1986.

Stowe, Harriet Beecher. *Uncle Tom's Cabin; or, Life among the Lowly.* 1852. Ed. Ann Douglas. New York: Penguin, 1981.

Tolles, Frederick B. "The Culture of Early Pennsylvania." *Pennsylvania Magazine of History and Biography* 81 (1957): 119–37.

———. *Meeting House and Counting House: The Quaker Merchants of Colonial Philadelphia, 1682–1763.* Chapel Hill: University of North Carolina Press, 1948.

———. *Quakers and the Atlantic Culture.* New York: Macmillan Company, 1960.

Tomes, Nancy. "The Quaker Connection: Visiting Patterns among Women in the Philadelphia Society of Friends, 1750–1800." *Friends and Neighbors: Group Life in*

America's First Plural Society. Ed. Michael Zuckerman. Philadelphia: Temple University Press, 1982. 174–95.

Tompkins, Jane. *Sensational Designs: The Cultural Work of American Fiction, 1790–1860.* New York: Oxford University Press, 1985.

Trattner, Walter I. *From Poor Law to Welfare State: A History of Social Welfare in America.* 2nd ed. New York: Free Press, 1979.

Tucker, George Fox. *A Quaker Home.* Boston: George B. Reed, 1891.

Ulrich, Laurel Thatcher. *Good Wives: Image and Reality in the Lives of Women in Northern New England, 1650–1750.* New York: Oxford University Press, 1980.

Vaughan, Alden, ed. *The Puritan Tradition in America, 1620–1730.* New York: Harper and Row, 1972.

Voss, Norine. "'Saying the Unsayable': An Introduction to Women's Autobiography." *Gender Studies: New Directions in Feminist Criticism.* Ed. Judith Spector. Bowling Green, Ohio: Popular Press, 1986. 218–33.

Watkins, Owen. "Some Early Quaker Autobiographies." *Journal of the Friends' Historical Society* 45 (Autumn 1953): 65–74.

Wells, Robert V. "Quaker Marriage Patterns in a Colonial Perspective." *William and Mary Quarterly* 29 (July 1972): 415–42.

———. "Women's Lives Transformed: Demographic and Family Patterns in America, 1600–1970." *Women of America: A History.* Ed. Carol Ruth Berkin and Mary Beth Norton. Boston: Houghton Mifflin, 1979. 16–33.

Weintraub, Karl J. "Autobiography and Historical Consciousness." *Critical Inquiry* 1 (June 1975): 821–48.

Whittier, John Greenleaf. *The Complete Poetical Works of Whittier.* The Cambridge Edition. Boston: Houghton Mifflin, 1894.

Woolman, John. *The Journal and Major Essays of John Woolman.* Ed. Phillips P. Moulton. Richmond, Ind.: Friends United Press, 1989.

Worrall, Arthur J. *Quakers in the Colonial Northeast.* Hanover, N.H.: University Press of New England, 1980.

Wright, Louis B. *The Cultural Life of the American Colonies, 1607–1763.* New York: Harper and Row, 1957.

Wright, Luella M. *The Literary Life of the Early Friends, 1650–1725.* New York: Columbia University Press, 1932.

Yoder, Don. "Pennsylvania's Plain Garb." *Pennsylvania Folklife* 12 (Summer 1962): 2–5.

Zuckerman, Michael, ed. *Friends and Neighbors: Group Life in America's First Plural Society.* Philadelphia: Temple University Press, 1982.

Index

DATE DUE